Ferdinand Van Derveer Garretson

Carmina Yalensia : a Complete and accurate Collection of

Yale College songs

with Piano accompaniment

Ferdinand Van Derveer Garretson

Carmina Yalensia : a Complete and accurate Collection of Yale College songs
with Piano accompaniment

ISBN/EAN: 9783744789561

Printed in Europe, USA, Canada, Australia, Japan

Cover: Foto ©Thomas Meinert / pixelio.de

More available books at **www.hansebooks.com**

CARMINA YALENSIA:

A COMPLETE AND ACCURATE COLLECTION OF

YALE COLLEGE SONGS

WITH

PIANO ACCOMPANIMENT

COMPILED AND ARRANGED BY

FERD. V. D. GARRETSON.

NEW YORK:

Published by TAINTOR BROTHERS & Co., No. 229 Broadway.

PREFACE.

THE design of this volume of YALE SONGS is to supply a manifest deficiency in the compilations of the College.

The stranger who has been amused and entertained by the gusto with which our songs are sung, has naturally wished to procure a collection of them ; but his inquiries have hitherto been in vain, as many of the tunes now, for the first time, presented to the public, had never been written or arranged, but simply sung traditionally on the jolly occasions and festivals of college life.

The editor having gleaned the most popular, and those embodying the Yale spirit, words and customs, takes pleasure in presenting them to the musical world.

In this connection the Editor would make acknowledgements to different members of the college for the readiness with which they have rendered invaluable assistance in the collection of materials for this volume, and especially to Mr. CHAS. S. ELLIOT, of the class of '67, who has had immediate supervision in the arrangement of much of the music.

FERD. V. D. GARRETSON.

YALE THEOLOGICAL SEMINARY,
June 1, 1867.

WARREN, Music Stereotyper, 43 Centre-st. New York

CONTENTS.

For Index of First Lines see Page 88.

CARMINA YALENSIA.

INTEGER VITÆ.

Lib. I. Ode XXII. Q Horatii Flacci.

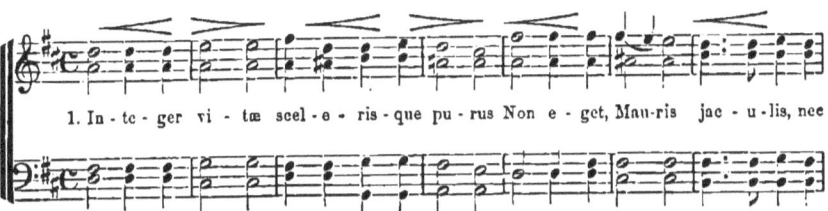

1. In - te - ger vi - tæ scel - e - ris - que pu - rus Non e - get, Man-ris jac - u - lis, nec

ar - cu, Nec ve - ne - na - tis grav-i - da sa - git - tis, Fus - ce pha-re - tra ;

2 Sive per Syrtes iter æstuosas,
Sive facturus per inhospitalem
Caucasum, vel quæ loca fabulosus
Lambit Hydaspes,

4 Namque me silva lupus in Sabina,
Dum meam canto Lalagen, et ultra
Terminum curis vagor expeditus,
Fugit inermem :

4 Quale portentum neque militaris
Daunias latis alit æsculetis,

Nec Jubæ tellus generat, leonum
Arida nutrix.

5 Pone me, pigris ubi nulla campis
Arbor æstiva recreatur aura,
Quod latus mundi nebulæ malusque
Jupiter urget.

6 Pone sub curru nimium propinqui
Solis, in terra domibus negata ;
Dulce ridentem Lalagen amabo
Dulce loquentem.

CARMINA YALENSIA.

INTEGER VITÆ.

Lib. I. Ode XXII, Q Horatii Flacci.

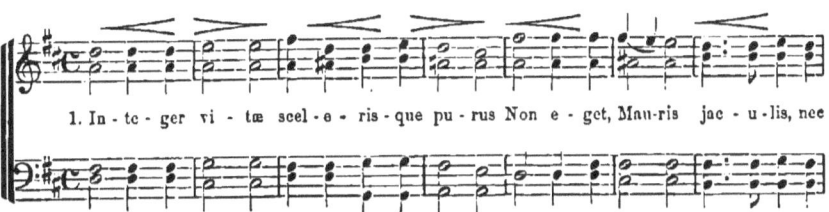

1. In - te - ger vi - tæ scel - e - ris - que pu - rus Non e - get, Mau - ris jac - u - lis, nec

ar - cu, Nec ve - ne - na - tis grav - i - da sa - git - tis, Fus - ce pha - re - tra;

2 Sive per Syrtes iter æstuosas,
Sive facturus per inhospitalem
Caucasum, vel quæ loca fabulosus
Lambit Hydaspes,

4 Namque me silva lupus in Sabina,
Dum meam canto Lalagen, et ultra
Terminum curis vagor expeditus,
Fugit inermem :

4 Quale portentum neque militaris
Daunias latis alit æsculetis,

Nec Jubæ tellus generat, leonum
Arida nutrix.

5 Pone me, pigris ubi nulla campis
Arbor æstiva recreatur aura,
Quod latus mundi nebulæ malusque
Jupiter urget.

6 Pone sub curru nimium propinqui
Solis, in terra domibus negata ;
Dulce ridentem Lalagen amabo
Dulce loquentem.

Allegretto scherzando.

1. Yale College is a jol-ly home; Swe-de-le-we-dum-bum, We love it still, where-

'er we roam, Swe-delewe-dumbum *mf* The ve-ry songs we used to sing, Swedeleweetchu-

DUET.

hi-ra-sa, 'Mid memory's ech-oes long shall ring, Swe-delewe-dumbum

CHORUS.
FIRST AND SECOND TENOR.

ff Li-to-ri-a! Li-to-ri-a! Swe-de-lewetchuhirasa! Li-to-ri-a! Li-to-ri-a! Swedelewedumbum.

FIRST AND SECOND BASS.

2 As Freshmen first we come to Yale:
Examinations make us pale.
But when we reach our Senior year,
Of such things we have lost our fear.
Chorus.

3 As Sophomores we have a task—
'Tis best performed with torch and mask—
For Euclid dead the Students weep,
And bury him while Tutors sleep.
Chorus.

4 In Junior Year we study French ;
Roberti pleads to an empty bench.
When college life begins to swoon,
It drinks new life from the Wooden Spoon.
Chorus.

5 As Seniors we all take our ease,
We smoke our pipes and sing our glees.
The saddest tale we have to tell,
Is when we bid our friends farewell !
Chorus.

6 And then into the world we come :
We've made good friends and studied some.
And till the Sun and Moon shall pale
We'll love and rev'rence Mother Yale.
Chorus.

——

WOODEN SPOON SONG.

BY JOHN E. KIMBALL, '58.

AIR—" *Litoria.*"

1 Let bards in strains of triumph sing,
The glories of the Battle-King,
Our homage claims that *valiant* Jun'—
The Hero of the Wooden Spoon.
Chorus—Litoria ! Litoria !

2 Let laurels deck the titled sage,
And greener grow from age to age,
To fade before that *sapient* Jun'—
The Hero of the Wooden Spoon.
Chorus.

3 Let knights their hostile lances break,
And dare it for their ladies' sake,
But quail before that *gallant* Jun'—
The Hero of the Wooden Spoon.
Chorus.

4 Then wreathe the ivy, swell the song,
Ring out the chorus loud and long,
With *three times three* for that *brave* Jun'—
The Hero of the Wooden Spoon.

——

OLD YALE.

BY J. K. LOMBARD, '54.

AIR—" *The Brave Old Oak.*"

1 A song for old Yale, for brave old Yale,
Who hath stood in her glory long—
Here's honor and fame to her reverend name
And the mem'ries that round it throng.
There's a thrill in the word that the heart hath
stirred,
Though breathed in a maiden's sigh,
But as wild, on the gale rings the rally of
' Yale,'
And stern, as a battle-cry.
Then sing to old Yale, to brave old Yale,
Who stands in her pride alone,
And still flourish she, like a hale green tree,
When a thousand years have flown.

2 In the days of old, when our father's bold
To the hills and the forests came—
At their altar-fires kindled high desires
In a pure and holy flame.
'Mid the towering wood like a stripling stood,
Now so hearty and strong and hale,
Where for ages shall stand as the pride of the
land,
And guardian of liberty,—Yale.
Then sing to old Yale, to brave old Yale,
Who stands in her pride alone,
And still flourish she, like a hale green tree,
When a thousand years have flown.

3 In the soft Southern clime and the Arctic
rime,
By river and valley and dell,
Where wanderers roam and man finds a
home,
There her myriad offspring dwell ;
And the chorus of praise which together they
raise
Comes sounding from mountain and vale—
" Till life's sun is set we will never forget
But honor and cherish old Yale."
Then sing to old Yale, to brave old Yale,
Who stands in her pride alone,
And still flourish she, like a hale green tree,
When a thousand years have flown.

ALMA MATER.

SOLO. *Allegretto.*

1. Al - ma Ma - ter! Al - ma Ma - ter! Heav'n's blessing attend thee, While we live we will

cherish, pro - tect and de - fend thee; Thy sons, dear old Yale, sing in loud, thrilling

cho - rus, While we think of thy great men who've been here be - fore us.

1st Tenor, *CHORUS.*
2d Tenor.
ƒƒ Hurrah! Hurrah! Alma Ma-ter for-ev-er. Hurrah! Hurrah! Alma Mater for-ev-er.
1st Base.
2d Base.

2 Alma Mater! Alma Mater! we ne'er shall
forget thee,
Embalmed in the shrine of our hearts have
we set thee;
Thou haven of rest in life's tempest-torn
ocean,
Where calmly we rode in youth's wildest
commotion.
Hurrah! hurrah! &c.

3 Alma Mater! Alma Mater! watch o'er our
last parting,
Wipe away those sad tears that too soon
may be starting;
Whisper thou o'er our doubts, "Duty calls
you, be brave,
Truth's soldier's are fainting, go, succor and
save.
Be brave—be true—your country will love you,
Be right—your might in God above you."

4 Alma Mater! Alma Mater! we'll bring to
thy shrine,
Our first fruits of Fame, let the offering be
thine;
You trained our young minds, and you
taught us to think,
From thy classic fountains, rich draughts
did we drink.
Hurrah! hurrah! &c.

5 Alma Mater! Alma Mater! ere we visit thee
more,
These elms may be falling, all moss-covered
o'er;
Yet we'll tread thy old halls, though with
ag'd footfall creeping,
Their echoes shall wake joys that only were
sleeping.
Hurrah! hurrah! &c.

POW-WOW SONG.

BY H. BINNEY, '59.

AIR — "*Alma Mater.*"

1 Alma Mater! Alma Mater! the moonlight
is shining,
On thy time-honored towers, where the ivy
is twining;
Thy tall elms are waving their green leaflets
o'er us,
As they waved o'er thy children in ages
before us.
Hurrah! hurrah! Alma Mater forever!

2 Alma Mater! Alma Mater! the lurid light
streaming
From our red flashing torches, is fitfully
gleaming;
Before us, the flames in the night breeze are
glancing,
And behind us the wavering shadows are
dancing.
Hurrah! hurrah! Alma Mater forever!

3 Alma Mater! Alma Mater! in harmony
meeting,
All the rites of thy Pow-Wow to-night
we're repeating;
Long honored remains of a past generation,
May they still be repeated at each Presenta-
tion!
Hurrah! hurrah! Alma Mater forever!

4 Alma Mater! Alma Mater! our pulses
throb lightly,
When we think of those blue eyes that o'er
shine brightly.
Entwined with our heart strings, like lover's
caresses,
Are the thoughts of soft glances, and bright,
sunny tresses.
Hurrah! hurrah! Alma Mater forever!

5 Alma Mater! Alma Mater! celebrated in
story,
Of Columbia's great empire the pride and
the glory,
We ne'er shall forget thee though years may
roll o'er us,
And to life's latest hour we'll remember the
chorus.
Hurrah! Fifty-Nine! Alma Mater forever!

2 Ubi sunt, qui ante nos
  In mundo fuere?
  Transeas ad superos,
  Abeas ad inferos,
    Quos si vis videre.

3 Vita nostra brevis est,
  Brevi finietur,
  Venit mors velociter,
  Rapit nos atrociter,
    Nemini parcetur.

4 Vivat academia,
  Vivant professores,
  Vivat membrum quodlibet,
  Vivant membra quælibet,
    Semper sint in flore.

5 Vivant omnes virgines,
  Faciles, formosæ,
  Vivant et mulieres,
  Teneræ amabiles,
    Bonæ laboriosæ.

6 Vivat et republica,
  Et qui illam regit,
  Vivat nostra civitas,
  Mæcenatum caritas,
    Quæ nos hic protegit.

7 Pereat tristitia,
  Pereant osores,
  Pereat diabolus,
  Quivis antiburschius,
    Atque irrisores.

8 Quis confluxus hodie
  Academicorum?
  E longinquo convenerunt
  Protinusque successerunt
    In commune forum.

9 Alma Mater floreat,
  Quæ nos educavit,
  Caros et commilitones,
  Dissitas in regiones
    Sparsos congregavit.

GAUDEAMUS.

TRANSLATED BY L. W. FITCH OF '40.

With two original stanzas.

AIR—" *Gaudeamus*."

1 Let us now in youth rejoice,
  None can justly blame us,
For when golden youth has fled,
And in age our joys are dead,
  Then the dust doth claim us.

2 Where have all our Fathers gone?
  Here we'll see them never:
Seek the gods' serene abode—
Cross the dolorous Stygian flood—
  · There they dwell for ever.

3 Brief is this our life on earth,
  Brief—nor will it tarry—
Swiftly death runs to and fro,
All must feel his cruel blow,
  None the dart can parry.

4 Raise we then the joyous shout,
  Life to Yale for ever!
Life to each Professor here;
Life to all our comrades dear,
  May they leave us never.

5 Life to all the maidens fair,
  Maidens sweet and smiling;
Life to gentle matrons, too,
Ever kind and ever true,
  All our cares beguiling.

6 May our land for ever bloom
  Under wise direction;
And this city's classic ground
In munificence abound,
  Yielding us protection.

7 Perish sadness, perish hate,
  And ye scoffers, leave us!
Perish every shape of woe,
Devil and Philistine too,
  That would fain deceive us.

ADDENDA.

1 Youth and hope a glory wear,
  While on earth they're given,
That immortals ever share
In the pure and balmy air
  Of the hills of heaven.

2 Let us then in youth rejoice,
  'Twill repent us never,
For when earthly scenes have fled,
And this mortal life is sped,
  Youth abides for ever.

INTRODUCTORY ODE.

BURIAL OF EUCLID.

CLASS OF '53.

TUNE—" *Gaudeamus*."

1 Fundite nunc lacrymas
  Plorate Yalenses,—
Euclid rapuerunt fata
Membra et ejus inhumata
  Linquimus tres menses.

2 Salvete vos, Sophomores,
  Fortes et audaces,—
Sidera clarissima,
Fulmina dirissima,
  Portantesque faces.

3 Vivat quisquis huc adest
  Auditum Sermones,—
Salvete vos Seniores
Salveteque Juniores—
  Salvete Tirones.

4 Surgite nunc, Liquidi,
  Carmen et cantemus,—
Fratres adhuc fuimus,
Fratres semper erimus,
  Vitam dum habemus.

5 Omnes Præses expellat,
  Facultas minetur,—
Nobis tamen fortiter
Funeri portabitur
  Euclid, et condetur.

6 Nullus non deficiat
  Funeri qui venit;
Semper omnis et ruens
Quatuor et obtinens,
  Attagenæ cœnat.

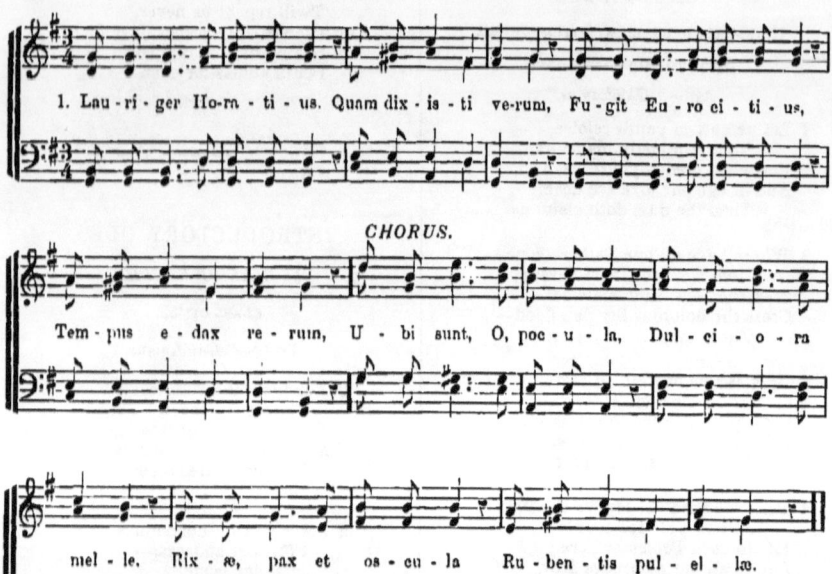

1. Lau - ri - ger Ho - ra - ti - us. Quam dix - is - ti ve-rum, Fu - git Eu - ro ci - ti - us,

CHORUS.

Tem - pus e - dax re - rum, U - bi sunt, O, poc - u - la, Dul - ci - o - ra

mel - le. Rix - æ, pax et os - cu - la Ru - ben - tis pul - el - læ.

2 Crescit uva molliter,
   Et puella crescit,
   Sed poeta turpiter,
   Sitiens canescit.   *Cho.*

3 Quid juvat æternitas
   Nominis; amare
   Nisi terræ filias
   Licet, et potare !   *Cho.*

BIENNIAL JUBILEE SONG.

BY C. S. KELLOGG, '58.

AIR.—" *Lauriger Horatius.*"

1 Anni pleni gaudiis
   Jam duo volvere ;
   Tamen non tristitiis
     Semper caruere.
     CHORUS.   Summa voce canite
          O fratres amati,
          Et clamantes, hilare
          Simus nunc beati.

2 Clara sunt præterita
   Erunt et futura ;
   Ac Biennialia
   Exierunt dura.   *Cho.*

3 Licet nobis liberis
   Sub ulmis sedere
   Non coactis, asperis
   Legibus parere.   *Cho.*

4 Nostra facta gloria
   Semper coronabit,
   Ejus et memoria
   Posteris juvabit.   *Cho.*

5 Mali et immunitas
   Nobis remanebit,
   Et æterna unitas
   Inter nos valebit.   *Cho.*

BROTHERS CAMPAIGN SONG.

BY JOHN M. HOLMES, '57.

AIR—"*Lauriger Horatius.*"

1 Brothers all in Unity,
  Knit by Love's attraction,
  Let us gird our armor on,
  Now's the time for action.
    Shake the old blue banner out,
    Tell the world its story,
    Let our song and watchword be,
    Unity and glory

2 Let the fires of Auld Lang Syne
  In all hearts be burning,
  Fires of friendship, eloquence,
  Liberty and Learning.   *Chorus.*

3 Gather in the candidates,
  Golden time is fleeting,
  Give to each a brother's right,
  Give a brother's greeting.   *Chorus.*

4 Shall we basely bend the knee
  To Linonia? NEVER!
  Hand in hand we'll firmly stand,
  Victorious forever.   *Chorus.*

LINONIA SONG.

AIR—"*Lauriger Horatius.*"

1 "Brothers all in Unity,"
  Mourning to distraction,
  Sitting around with faces *blue*,
  Waiting strength for action.
Chorus—With their "old blue banner down—
    Sobbing out the story,
    "This is all that's left behind
    Of David Humphrey's glory."

2 While beneath their banner blue
  Brother hosts draw near us;
  To Linonia's standard true,
  Soon that host will fear us.
    And their banner, in their flight,
    Shall tell the mournful story:
    "This is all that's left behind
    Of David Humphrey's glory."

8 "Linonia," invincible,
  Can whene'er she pleases,
  Pull that "old blue banner" down,
  And tear it all to pieces.

Pull that "old blue banner" down,
  And tell the world the story;
"This is all that's left behind
  Of David Humphrey's glory."

LAURIGER.

PARAPHRASED BY P. B. PORTER '67.

AIR—"*Lauriger.*"

1 Old man Horace, sprigged with bay,
  Truly you do say, sir,
  Time streaks faster on his way,
  Than *two-forty* racer.
  Chorus—Give us but our rum to sip;
    We don't care a clam-shell,
    So we kiss the pouting lip
    Of the blooming damsel.

2 With bright beauty blush the grapes;—
  So the women show it;
  Longing for their lovely shapes,
  Sings the tipsy poet.   *Chorus.*

3 Tell me what great fame avails,
  Save we can hug tightly
  All the jolly little quails,
  And get somewhat *slightly.*   *Chorus.*

LAURIGER.

TRANSLATED BY L. W. FITCH, '40.

AIR—"*Lauriger.*"

1 Poet of the laurel wreath,
  Horace, true thy saying;
"Time outstrips the tempest's breath;
  For no mortal staying."
Chorus—Bring me cups that Bacchus crowns,
    Cups on mirth attending;
    Give me blushing maidens' frowns,
    Frowns in kisses ending.

2 Sweetly grows the grape, the maid,
  Each in beauty peerless;
  But to me, bereft and sad,
  Wintry age comes cheerless.   *Chorus.*

3 Though enduring fame be mine,
  This shall yield no pleasure;
  Let me then, in love and wine,
  Find exhaustless treasure.   *Chorus.*

Presto.

f 1. As I was walking down the street, Heigho, heigho, heigho, heigho, A pret-ty girl I
    2. Said I to her, "What is your trade?" Heigho, heigho. heigho, heigho, Said she to me, "I'm a

chanced to meet, heigho, heigho, heigho. Rig-a-jig-jig, and a-way we go, a-
weaver's maid, heigho, heigho, heigho. Rig-a-jig-jig, and a-way we go, etc.

way we go, a-way we go, Rig-a-jig-jig, and a-way we go heigho, heigho, heigh-

o, heigho, heigho, heigho, heigho, heigho, heigho, heigho, heigho.

Rig-a-jig-jig, and a-way we go, Heigh-o, heigh-o, heigh-o.

BROTHERS' CAMPAIGN SONG. (IL PURITANI.) 15

By H. A. Brown, '65.

Alla Marcia.

1. Brothers, now the time has come, To win un-dy-ing fame, To add new, brighter
Chorus. Unfurl, un-furl that ban-ner blue, O! wave that flag on high. Loud let our conquering

lus - tre, To Bro-thers' glorious name. Fortune, fickle though she be, Smiles always on the
paeans ring, Our mot - to, vic-to - ry...

brave,.... And vic-t'ry ev - er fol-lows on Where'er their banners wave. Hurrah!

2 Now new figures gather round
  'Neath the wide spread elms,
Soon to join our happy band
  In dear Yalensian realms ;
Meet them with a cordial grasp—
  Bring them to our hall,
Where Love and Friendship, Joy and Truth,
  In unity bind all—Hurrah !
  Cho. Unfurl, unfurl that banner, etc.

3 Onward then bound heart to heart,
  Brothers loved we go ;
With one accord we proudly shout
  Defiance to the foe.
Across life's trackless, stormy sea,
  We hopefully set sail,
Undaunted 'midst the raging waves,
  The lightning and the gale—Hurrah !
Cho. Nail to the mast that banner blue ;—
  O ! wave our flag on high,
  Loud let our conquering paeans ring
  Our motto, victory !

LINONIA CAMPAIGN SONG.

BY S. W. DUFFIELD, '63.

AIR.—"*Il Puritani.*"

1 Honored in song and story
  Fairest of queens, to thee

Higher, far higher glory,
  And nobler praises yet shall be.
Thine be the cheerful chorus
  Which rises through the sky
Ringing, while still before us
  The conquered foemen fly—they fly.
Cho. Then be the honor ever
    Linonia's alone ;
  She reigns supreme, and never
  Shall leave her ancient throne.

2 Bright glows the red of morning,
  But brighter shines the red
Over the field, adorning
  The banner of our hope o'erhead.
After that waving token,
  Victorious in fight,
March we in rank unbroken,
  Prepared to hold our right—our right.
Cho. Then be the honor ever, etc.

3 Clearer, as seasons vanish,
  Glitters her spotless name ;
Years pass and never banish
  The memory of her cherished fame,
And as of old we crowned her,
  With wreaths of woven bay,
Cast we once more around her
  The laurels won to-day—to-day.
Cho. Then be the honor ever, etc.

2 The leaf burns bright, like the gems of light,
   That flash in the braids of Beauty,
It nerves each heart for the hero's part,
   On the battle plain of duty.

3 In the thoughtful gloom of his darkened
   room,
   Sits the child of song and story,
But his heart is light, for his pipe beams
   bright,
   And his dreams are all of glory.

4 By the blazing fire sits the gray-haired sire,
   And infant arms surround him ;
And he smiles on all in that quaint old hall,
   While the smoke-curls float around him.

5 In the forest grand of our native land,
   When the savage conflict's ended,
The " Pipe of Peace" brought a sweet re-
   lease
   From toil and terror blended.

6 The dark-eyed train of the maids of Spain,
   'Neath their arbor shades trip lightly,
And a gleaming cigar, like a new born star,
   In the clasp of their lips burns brightly.

7 It warms the soul, like the blushing bowl,
   With its rose-red burden streaming,
And drowns it in bliss, like the first warm
   kiss
   From the lips with love-buds teeming.

   Then smoke away till a golden ray
     Lights up the dawn of the morrow,
   For a cheerful cigar, like a shield will bar
     The blows of care and sorrow.

ALUMNI SONG.

BY F. M. FINCH, '49.

Air— " *Sparkling and bright* "

1 Gather ye smiles from the ocean isles,
   Warm hearts from river and fountain,
A playful chime from the palm tree clime,
   From the land of rock and mountain ;
   And roll the song in waves along,
     For the hours are bright before us,
   And grand and hale are the elms of Yale,
     Like fathers, bending o'er us.

2 Summon our band from the prairie land,
   From the granite hills, dark frowning,
From the lakelet blue and the black bayou,
   From the snows our pine peaks crowning;
   And pour the song in joy along,
     For the hours are bright before us,
   And grand and hale are the towers of
     Yale,
     Like giants, watching o'er us.

3 Count not the tears of the long gone years,
   With their moments of pain and sorrow,
But laugh in the light of their memories
   bright,
   And treasure them all for the morrow.
   Then roll the song in waves along,
     While the hours are bright before us.
   And high and hale are the spires of Yale,
     Like guardians, towering o'er us.

4 Dream of the days when the rainbow rays
   Of Hope, on our hearts fell lightly,
And each fair hour some cheerful flower
   In our pathway blossomed brightly ;
   And pour the song in joy along
     Ere the moments fly before us,
   While portly and hale the sires of Yale
     Are kindly gazing o'er us.

5 Linger again in memory's glen,
   'Mid the tendril vines of feeling,
Till a voice or a sigh floats softly by,
   Once more to the glad heart stealing ;
   And ro l the song in waves along,
     For the hours are bright before us,
   And in cottage and vale are the brides
     of Yale,
     Like angels, watching o'er us.

6 Clasp ye the hand 'neath the arches grand
   That with garlands span our greeting,
With a silent prayer that an hour as fair
   May smile on each after meeting ;
   And long may the song, the joyous song
     Roll on in the hours before us,
   And grand and hale may the elms of
     Yale
     For many a year bend o'er us.

LINONIA. (CRAMBAMBULI.)

Words by F. M. FINCH, '49.

Allegro.

I Li-no-ni-a, the wreaths of glo-ry Sit lightly on thy peer-less brow... With graceful song, and thril-ling sto-ry, Thy name and praise are woven now... Then brothers, let the loud huzza, Re-e-cho for Li-no-ni-a. Long live Li-no-ni-a, Li-no-ni-a!

2 From northern rock and southern valley,
From crystal lake and prairie land,
Her children, at her summons rally
And gather round her, hand in hand.
  Then let it ring—the loud huzza,
  For gallant, gay Linonia!
Long live Linonia—Linonia!

3 On Senate floor and field of battle,
Her sons have struck the patriot's blow ;
Nor foreign threat, nor musket rattle,
Could bend their noble spirits low.
  Then proudly shout huzza, huzza!
  Our hearts are thine, Linonia!
Long live Linonia—Linonia !

4 Her ancient halls have oft resounded
With shout and song of victory:
By warm and fearless hearts surrounded,
Her banners all wave merrily.
  Then onward, all ! huzza, huzza!
  Fight bravely for Linonia!
Long live Linonia—Linonia!

5 Along the patient path of duty,
Her voice shall cheer our weary way;
Beneath the trustful smile of beauty,
Our thoughts to her shall often stray;
  And ere our children lisp "mamma,"
  We'll make them sing Linonia,
Long live Linonia—Linonia!

6 Then, brothers, let the swelling chorus
Our mingled pride and joy proclaim;
Linonia's shield is blazing o'er us,
It lights the winding path of fame.
  Then let it ring—the proud huzza!
  Three cheers for brave Linonia!
Long live Linonia—Linonia!

AUDACIA.

BY C. G. CAME, '59.

AIR — " *Crambambuli.*"

1 Audacia, this is the title
  Of that good trait we love the best;
  It is the means which proves most vital,
  When evil fortunes us molest;
  Against all troubles near and far,
  I seek thy aid—Audacia.

2 Go I into the recitation,
  Most like some urchin cavilier;
  I banish doubt and hesitation,
  And meet all boring with a sneer!
  I vex the tutor, ha! ha! ha!
  And plague him with—Audacia.

3 And am I pleased with rosy slumber,
  Or have I business of my own,
  Excuses rise—a countless number,
  Which for the absence may atone;
  I make a cold, or sad catarrh,
  Present it with—Audacia.

4 Did I possess the lofty station
  Of our dear Prex., so good and bright,
  On sheep-skins at the graduation,
  This motto would I ever write:
  " Vobiscum pertinacia
  Uti semper Audacia."

5 Do parents send a solemn letter,
  Made wiser by the Faculty,
  And gravely speak of actions better,
  Of virtue, laws, and piety?
  How dutiful I write my ma
  Right filial with—Audacia.

6 But do not think our life is aimless,
  Oh no, we crave one blessed boon,
  It is the prize of value nameless,
  The honored, classic wooden spoon;
  But give us this, we'll shout hurrah!
  Oh, nothing like—Audacia.

7 Ye plodders dull in all the classes,
  Your sad condition we deplore;
  In knowledge's road ye are but asses,
  While we our ponies ride before;
  Ho! clear the track, and flee afar,
  Make way for bold—Audacia.

8 Audacia! it still shall bear me
  Along the rugged path of life;
  For every scene it shall prepare me,
  At least it must procure a wife;
  Then onward to life's earnest war,
  Lead on the charge—Audacia.

DRY UP.

BY I. RILEY, '58.

AIR— " *Crambambuli.*"

1 As down the tide of time we're rowing,
  One song we'll sing with right good will;
  We'll wake the echoes while we're going,
  And sing " Dry up!" to every ill.
  Then boatmen sing it loud and long,
  And shout the chorus stout and strong,
  Dry up! shall be the song, dry up! dry up!

2 Whene'er the chapel bell is swinging
  And tinkling in the frosty morn,
  We waken with the dismal ringing,
  And ponder at our fate forlorn.
  We pull the coverlid high up,
  And grumbling, growl, dry up! dry up!
  Dry up! we say, dry up! dry up! dry up!

3 If e'er, unfortunately smitten
  By passion for some faithless fair,
  From her we get the mystic " mitten,"
  We'll sing, " dry up!" but never swear.
  Though visions of the " silver cup,"
  Should thus be turned the wrong side
      up,
  Who cares while we can sing, dry up!
      dry up!

4 When tailors bring us bills for breeches,
  And gravely talk of needed cash,
  We tell them, as our pocket itches,
  Politely, they may go to smash.
  We roll the whites of each eye up,
  And muttering, sing to them, dry up!
  Dry up! we sing, dry up! dry up! dry up!

5 We fell upon that dread Biennial,
  With mighty blows and lusty kicks,
  And now at last to joys perennial,
  Were sculled with *Bohns* across the Styx.
  So now by morning, night and noon,
  Whenever sings a jolly Jun',
  Dry up! shall be the tune, dry up! dry up!

6 No gloomy clouds shall dim his vision
  Who sings, dry up! to all his woes;
  But hastening on to joys Elysian,
  These words will cheer him as he goes.
  Then give all grief and sighing up,
  And put your trust in drying up,
  And gaily sing, dry up! dry up! dry up!

1. Come, classmates, gather round us now, And swell our joy-ous song; Let care be banished

from each brow, While time speeds swift along. We're thro' the toils of Soph'more year, We've passed the Rubi-

- con, There's noth-ing left to give us fear, Bi-en-ni-al is done.

CHORUS.

Bi-en-ni-al is done, Biennial is done, There's nothing left to give us fear, Biennial is done.

2 The years to come may bring sad care—
Let come when come it may—
To-day the sky above is fair,
So now let all be gay ;
And when the clouds shall come at last,
As come full sure they will,
We'll think of all our pleasures past,
And so be happy still !
And so be happy still, &c.

3 Two years have gone since first we met,
In friendship firm we're bound ;
In those to come we'll ne'er forget
The friends that now are round.
So pledging here with heart and hand,
Together still to strive,
We meet a happy, loving band—
The Class of Fifty-Five !
The class of Fifty-Five, &c.

4 Hither we came with hearts of joy, with joy
we now will part,
And give to each the parting grasp which
speaks a brother's heart,
United firm in pleasing words, which can no
breaking know,
For Sons of Yale can ne'er forget their Alma
Mater O—
Oh ! Alma Mater O, &c.

5 Then brush the tear-drop from your eye,
and happy let us be,
For oy alone should fill the hearts of those as
blest as we ;
One cheerful chorus, ringing loud, we'll give
before we go,
The memory of college days and Alma Mater
O—
Oh ! Alma Mater O, Alma Mater O,
Hurrah ! hurrah ! for college days and Alma
Mater O.

PARTING SONG.

Air—"*Benny Havens.*"

1 We're gathered now, my class-mates, to join
our parting song,
To pluck from memory's wreath the buds
which there so sweetly throng ;
To gaze on life's broad ruffled sea, to which
we quickly go,
But ere we start we'll drink the health of
Alma Mater O—
Chorus.
Oh ! Alma Mater O, Oh ! Alma Mater O—
But ere we start we'll drink the health of
Alma Mater O.

2 No more for us yon tuneful bell shall ring
for morning prayers,
No more to long Biennial we'll mount yon
attic stairs ;
Our recitations all are passed—Alumnuses you
know,
We'll swell the praises long and loud of Alma
Mater O—
Oh ! Alma Mater O, &c.

3 We go to taste the joys of life, like bubbles
on its tide,
Now glittering in its sunbeams and dancing in
their pride,
But bubble like they'll break and burst, and
leave us sad, you know,
There's none so sweet as memory of Alma
Mater O—
Oh ! Alma Mater O, &c.

AUREM PRÆBE MIHI.

Air—"*We'll dance by the light of the Moon.*"

1 Felis sedit by a hole,
Intenta she cum omni soul,
Prendere rats.
Mice cucurrunt over the floor,
In numero, duo, tres or more,
Obliti cats.

2 Felis saw them oculis,
"I'll have them," inquit she, "I guess,
Dum ludunt."
Tunc illa crept toward the group,
"Habeam," dixit, "good rat soup !
Pingues sunt !"

3 Mice continued all ludere,
Intenti in ludum vere,
Gaudent r.
Tunc rushed the felis unto them,
Et tore them omnes limb from limb,
Violenter.

MORAL.

Mures, omni mice be shy,
Et aurem præbe mihi,
Benigne ;
Si hoc fuges, verbum sat,
Avoid a huge and hungry cat,
Studiose.

UPIDEE.

CHORUS.   *SOLO.*

I. The shades of night were falling fast, Upi-dee, Upi - da, As through an Alpine village passed

CHORUS.   *SOLO.*   *ritard.*

Upi - dee - i - da! A youth, who bore, 'mid snow and ice, A banner with the strange device,

CHORUS.

U - pi - dee - i, dee - i, da, U - pidee, U - pada, U - pi - dee - i, dee i, da,

U - pi - dee - i - da! * r-r-r-r-r-r-r-r-r-r-r-r-r-r-r-r r-r-r-r-r-r-r-ryah'yah!yah!yah

The n must be strongly rolled.

U - pi-dee - i dee-i - da, U - pi-dee, U - pi - da, U - pi-dee - i, dee - i, da, U - pi-dee - i - da!

2 His brow was sad; his eye beneath
Flashed like a faulchion from its sheath,
And like a silver clarion rung
The accents of that unknown tongue,
Upideei, &c.

3 "O stay," the maiden said, "and rest
Thy weary head upon this breast!"
A tear stood in his bright blue eye,
But still he answered with a sigh
Upideei, &c.

4 At break of day, as heavenward
The pious monks of Saint Bernard
Uttered the oft repeated prayer,
A voice cried through the startled air,
Upideei, &c.

5 A traveller, by the faithful hound,
Half buried in the snow was found,
Still grasping in his hand of ice
That banner with the strange device,
Upideei, &c.

AIR. UPIDEE.

1 The shades of night were a-comin' down swift,
And the snow was a-heapin' up drift on drift;
Through a Yankee village a youth did go,
Carryin' a flag with this motto:
Cho. Upidee, &c.

2 O'er his high forehead curled copious hair,
He'd a Roman nose, and complexion fair;
He'd a bright blue eye, and an auburn lash,
And he ever kept a-shoutin' through his moustache. —Cho.

3 "Oh, dont go up," said an old man, "stop!
It's blowing gales up there on top,
You'll tumble off on the t'other side,"
But the hurrying stranger still replied.—Cho.

4 "Oh, dont go up such a shocking bad night.
Come rest in this lap," said a maiden bright;
A tear on his Roman nose did come,
But still he remarked, as upward he clumb.—Cho.

5 "Look out for the branch of the sycamore tree,
Dodge the rolling stones if any you see;"
So saying the farmer went to bed
But that singular voice replied overhead:—Cho.

6 He saw through the windows as he kept a-gettin'
upper,
A number of families sitting at supper;
He eyed those slippery rocks very keen,
But fled as he cried, and cried while a - fleein:—
Cho.

7 About quarter-past six the next forenoon,
A man accidentally going up soon,
Heard spoken above him as much as twice,
These very same words, in a very weak voice :—
Cho.

8 Not far, I believe, from a quarter of seven,
He was slow getting up, the road being uneven;
He found buried up in the snow and ice,
The boy and the flag with the strange device:—
Cho.

9 Yes, he's dead, defunct, without any doubt,
The lamp of his life entirely gone out,
On the drear hill-side the youth was a - layin'.
And there was no more use for him to be a say-
in'.—Cho.

f Alla marcia.

1. Here's to good old Yale, drink it down,   Here's to good old Yale, drink it down,

drink it down,   drink it down,

FINE·

Here's to good old Yale, She's so hearty and so hale, Drink it down, drink it down, drink it down, down, down,

p   *cres.*

Balm of Gi- le- ad, Gi- le- ad, Balm of Gi- le- ad, Gi- le- ad, Balm of Gi- le- ad, Way

down on the Bin- go farm, *f* We won't go home a- ny more We won't go home a- ny more, We

won't go home a- ny more, Way down on the Bin-go farm, *p* Bingo, Bin-go, Bin-go, Bin-go,

cres.   D. C.

Bin- go, Bin-go, Way down on the Bin- go farm. *ff* (*Spoken.*)   O.

1. As Freshmen, first we come to Yale, Fol de rol do rol rol rol, Ex-am-i-nations make us pale, Fol de rol de rol rol rol.

Eel - i - eel - i - eel - i - Yale, Fol de rol de rol rol rol,

Eel - i - eel - i - eel - i - Yale Fol de rol de rol rol rol.

2 As Sophomores we have a task
'Tis best performed by torch and mask. *Cho.*

3 In Junior year we take our ease,
We smoke our pipes and sing our glees. *Cho.*

4 In Senior year we act our parts
In making love, and winning hearts. *Cho.*

5 And then into the world we come,
We're made good friends, and studied—some. *Cho.*

Adagio. 6 The saddest tale we have to tell,
Is when we bid our friends farewell. *Cho.*

*Eel-i-Yale; in honor of Elihu, or "Eli," Yale, the patron of Yale college.

2 I wish I was on yonder hill,
  For there I'd sit and cry my fill,
  And every drop should turn a mill,
  Dis cum bibble lolla boo.   Slow reel.
  Chorus.

3 I wish I was a married man,
  And had a wife whose name was Fan,
  I'd sing her a song on this same plan,
  Dis cum bibble lolla boo.   Slow reel.
  Chorus.

SONG OF THE SILVER-CUP.

BY J. W. HOOKER, '54.

AIR— *" Shool."*

1 We meet again, old Fifty-four,
  Just as jolly as of yore ;
  To smoke, laugh, joke, and sing once more,
  Dis cum bibble lolla boo.   Slow reel.

*Chorus—*Shool, shool, shool, I rool,
        Shool I shack a rack, shool a bar-
        bacool,
        The first time I saw psilly bally eel
        Dis cum bibble lolla boo.   Slow reel.

2 If there was one peculiar thing
  Our Class *could* do, it was to sing,
  Led off by White, and Weld, and Wing,
  Dis cum bibble lolla boo.   Slow reel.   *Cho.*

3 We serenaded every belle,—
  Miss Dutton many a tale could tell,
  Of noisy crowds around her well,
  Dis cum bibble lolla boo.   Slow reel.   *Cho.*

4 A funny Class was ours, they say,
  Split up and twisted every way ;
  Point out the splits, and twists to-day,
  Dis cum bibble lolla boo.   Slow reel.   *Cho.*

5 We've come from many a town and city :
  From Astley Cooper, Dwight, and Chitty ;
  But some *regret*—the more's the pity,
  Dis cum bibble lolla boo.   Slow reel.   *Cho.*

6 Friend Horton—lucky man is he,
  As ever signed himself A. B. ;
  He trots *our* baby on *his* knee,
  Dis cum bibble lolla boo.   Slow reel.   *Cho.*

7 God bless our first-born baby boy,
  May not one drop of sad alloy
  Be mingled in his *cup* of joy,
  Dis cum bibble lolla boo.   Slow reel.   *Cho.*

8 Bless all the babies, short and tall,
  Those that do and do not bawl ;
  Would we could only *cup* them all,
  Dis cum bibble lolla boo.   Slow reel.   *Cho.*

9 I wish I was a married man,
  Had followed out —— ——'s plan ;
  I mean to do it—if I can,
  Dis cum bibble lolla boo.   Slow reel.   *Cho.*

SONG.

BY JOHN MILTON HOLMES, '57.

AIR— *" Ellen Bayne."*

1 Soft eyes are dreaming
    Round us to-night,
  Tenderly gleaming,
    Floating in light.
  Born 'mid the brightness,
    Plainly I see
  Love from her ambush,
    Aiming at me.

*Chorus—*Welcome be those starry eyes,
      Clothed in beauty's magic guise ;
      Bidding joy and mirth arise—
      Dreaming of me.

2 Sweet smiles are wreathing
    Fair lips to-night,
  Lips that are breathing
    The spirit's delight,
  Telling of gladness,
    Telling of glee ;
  O ! that their music
    Murmured for me.

*Chorus—*Welcome be the fairy smile,
      Charming with its magic wile,
      Yet without a thought of guile,
      Beaming on me.

3 Warm hearts are beating
    Round us to-night,
  Giving to manhood
    Maidenly might—
  Away with foreboding,
    It cannot but be
  That some heart is waiting
    Somewhere for me.

*Chorus—*Welcome be that waiting heart,
      Loving truth and spurning art,
      Of my hope, my life, a part,
      Beating for me.

2 We have fought the fight together,
   We have struggled side by side;
Broken is the bond that held us,
   We must cut our sticks and slide.
   Chorus.

3 Some will go to Greece or Hartford,
   Some to Norwich or to Rome;
Some to Greenland's icy mountains,
   More, perhaps, will stay at home.
   Chorus.

4 When we come again together,
   Vigintennial to pass,
Wives and children all included—
   Won't we be an uproarious class?
   Chorus.

BIENNIAL JUBILEE SONG.

AIR—"*Cocachelunk.*"

1 Tell me not in mournful numbers,
   Of long nights of weary toil;
Broken and uneasy slumbers
   And the wasting "midnight oil,"

   Chorus—Cocachelunk chelunk chelaly,
      Cocachelunk chelunk chela,
      Cocachelunk chelunk chelaly,
      Hi! O, chickachelunk chela.

2 Tell me not of unshorn whiskers,
   Of each gloomy Sophomore,
Contemplating *Sophroniscus*,
   Cramming *Euclid* o'er and o'er.
   Chorus—Cocachelunk, &c.

3 Tell me not of old *Alcestis*,
   How she carried on of yore:
She forever now at rest is,
   Though she was a precious bore.
   Chorus—Cocachelunk, &c

4 Tell me not of fearful pleasures
   In the new Alumni Hall,
How the tutors brought forth treasures,
   Hidden till Biennial.
   Chorus—Cocachelunk, &c.

5 For Biennials are fleeting,
   And our hearts are stout and brave;
And to-day together meeting
   Sing we o'er our tyrants grave.
   Chorus—Cocachelunk &c.

6 But we did not wander blindly
   Through our Latin and our Greek;
Let us think a moment kindly
   Of our quadrupeds so sleek.
   Chorus—Cocachelunk, &c.

7 Through our labors swift they bore us,
   ("Bore us," not as tutors do,)
Singing here to-day our chorus,
   Think we of our *ponies* too,
   Chorus—Cocachelunk, &c.

8 But our cramming days are over,
   Gone are *Balbus, Euclid,*—all;
If we can, we will recover
   From that dread Biennial.
   Chorus—Cocachelunk, &c.

9 Bright the sky is beaming o'er us,
   Fresh and Soph'more years are o'er;
Juniors, join in singing chorus,
   Sing, "Biennials are a bore!"
   Chorus—Cocachelunk, &c.

PARTING SONG.

BY H. M. DUTTON, '57.
AIR—"*Ellen Bayne.*"

1 Burthened with fragrance,
   Breezes float by,
Laden with gladness,
   Hours o'er us fly;
Drown we our sorrow,
   In music and mirth,
This meeting may be
   Our last one on earth.
Chorus—Pleasant seem our college days,
   Dimmed by memory's golden haze,
   Be this last their brightest phase,
   Brothers of Yale!

2 Elms arching o'er us,
   Glorious and green,
Mellow the sunlight,
   Hallow the scene;
Fond arms of shadow,
   Round us they throw,
And tell of the future,
   Whispering low.   *Chorus.*

3 Brightly the future,
   Smiles on us now,
A vast summer ocean,
   Tempting the prow;
Leave we our dream life,
   Breaking the spell,
Clasp we our armor,
   Brothers! farewell.   *Chorus.*

1 'Twas off the blue Ca-na-ry isles, A glorious sum-mer day, I sat up-on the quarter deck, And whiffed my cares a-way; And as the volumed smoke arose, Like in-cense in the air, I breath'd a sigh to thinkin sooth, It was my last ci-gar.

CHORUS.

It was my last ci-gar, It was my last ci-gar, I breathed a sigh to think in sooth, It was my last ci-gar.

2 I leaned upon the quarter rail,
  And looked down in the sea,
E'en there the purple wreath of smoke
  Was curling gracefully,
Oh what had I at such a time,
  To do with wasting care,
Alas the trembling tear proclaimed
  It was my last Cigar.

3 I watched the ashes as it came
  Fast drawing toward the end,
I watched it as a friend would watch
  Beside a dying friend;
But still the flame crept slowly on,
  It vanished into air,
I threw it from me, spare the tale,
  It was my last Cigar.

4 I've seen the land of all I love
  Fade in the distance dim,
I've watched above the blighted heart,
  Where once proud hope hath been;
But I've never known a sorrow
  That could with that compare,
When off the blue Canaries,
  I smoked my last Cigar.

PARTING SONG.

BY GEO. S. DICKERMAN, '65.

AIR— "*Last Cigar.*"

1 Our tranquil day's last glimmering ray
  Fades o'er these cloister walls,
And with its flight the dim twilight
  Around us sadly falls,
While in the trees the whispering leaves
  Sing of the years now flown,
And cast their staid and sombre shade
  In gloomy silence down.

2 At this last hour, an unseen power
  Calls up with magic spell,
The hallowed ways of bygone days,
  To take our last farewell.
And lingering here, 'mid hope and fear,
  We look toward that unknown
Where in the strife of sterner life
  We each must war alone.

3 For here the road we long have trod,
  Breaks into untried ways,
And forth we roam into the gloom
  Of life's wild, clueless maze.
Then knit once more the bonds of yore,
  And grasp each proffered hand,
While memories bright our hearts unite,
  As here we waiting stand.

4 One love controls our hundred souls,
  One pulse in each beats high,
And one grief rests on every breast,
  At this, our last "good-by."
And though we part, in every heart
  One bond shall still survive,
While memory cheers the passing years,
  Old Yale and Sixty-Five.

PARTING SONG.

BY O. R. BURCHARD, '65.

AIR— "*Evening Bells.*"

1 The ev'ning of our College days,
  So swiftly passing, yet delays,
And draws its curt'ning twilight o'er
These College joys, we'll know no more
Save as their fading outlines rise
From mem'ry's page, before our eyes.

2 With sails unfurled we're on the stream
Which bears us onward, like a dream,
Into the great unknown of life,
Into the years of manly strife—
But yet a wreath of mem'ries dear
We'd twine to-day, our hearts to cheer.

3 We're leaving now this happy home,
In the wide future's fields to roam;
But ere we leave this pleasant land,
We'd stop to clasp the parting hand,
And with our brightest hopes in view,
Our pledge of friendship here renew.

4 If in life's toils our courage fail,
  We'll nerve our hearts with thoughts of
    Yale;
Or if the world should chance to lay
Upon our brows the victor's bay,
We'll place our honors on thy shrine,
Dear Alma Mater,—they are thine.

VIVE L'AMOUR.

Allegro molto. f

1. Let every good fellow now fill up his glass, Vive la compagnie, And drink to the health of our

glo-ri-ous class, Vi-ve la com-pagnie. *ff* Vive la, vive la, vive l'amour, Vive la, vive la,

Vi-ve l'a-mour, vi-ve l'a-mour, vi-ve l'a-mour, vi-ve la com-pag-nie.

2 Our Sophomore year is over and past,
   Vive la compagnie!
The *Day* of our sorrow has vanished at last,
   Vive la compagnie!

3 They spread us a table in Graduate's Hall,
   Vive la compagnie!
There one could get *board* for nothing at all,
   Vive la compagnie!

4 The meat was not meet for a student I own,
   Vive la compagnie!
'Twas plenty of skin with a good deal of Bohn,
   Vive la compagnie!

5 Here's health to the tutors who gave us good schemes,
   Vive la compagnie!
No smashes of sashes shall weaken their dreams,
   Vive la compagnie!

6 Here's health to the ladies whose beauty ne'er fad.s,
   Vive la compagnie!
A tutor apiece to all the old maids,
   Vive la compagnie!

7 Here's health to our class, so hearty and hale,
   Vive la compagnie!
Here's a health above all to our good mother YALE!
   Vive la compagnie!

BIENNIAL JUBILEE SONG.

Air—"*Vive L'Amour.*"

CLASS OF '67.

1 This day, my good fellows, Biennial 's o'er,
   Vive la '67;
We feel very sorry, but bewail him no more,
   Vive la '67.

Chorus—Vive la, vive la, vive la Yale,
   Vive la, vive la, vive la Yale,
   Vive la Yale, Vive la Yale,
   Vive la '67.

2 Let Mercury pass the bowl round the ring,
While we mournfully all the requiem sing.
   Chorus.

3 The blow was so sudden we feel quite bereaved
And as certain we are, the Greeks are *well greaved.*
   Chorus.

4 Let incense be offered, may the smoke of cigars,
Well sicken his spirit, 'way up in the stars.
   Chorus.

5 "*Old Sheridan's ride*" we now own will pale,
'Fore the *gallop* we took on our *ponies* at Yale.
   Chorus.

6 But time to the student wags swiftly by—
For nothing save pleasure scuds o'er his sky.
   Chorus.

DIRGE AT THE PYRE.

BURIAL OF EUCLID SONG.

CLASS OF '59.

AIR—"*Auld Lang Syne.*"

1 Old Euclid is departed now;
   Weep, weep, each Sophomore
The seal of death is on his brow,
   His *sphere* of life is o'er.

2 The flames in *circles* round him blaze,
   The torches o'er him shine;
And never more shall Euclid bore
   The class of Fifty-Nine.

3 Farewell, Old Euclid! Long for thee
   The tear of grief shall flow;
In plaintive song and *l. e. g.*,
   The world thy fame shall know.

4 When cramming Trigonometry,
   We'll think of auld lang *sine;*
For never more shall Euclid bore
   The class of Fifty-Nine.

34   IT'S A WAY WE HAVE AT OLD YALE.

A DRINKING SONG.

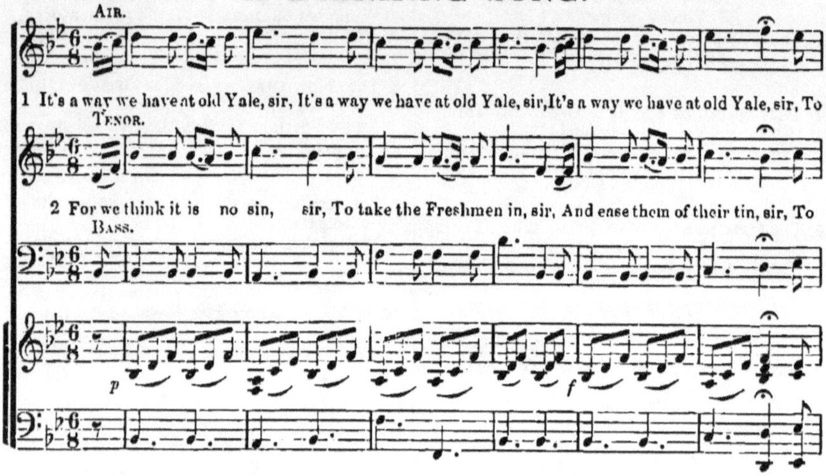

1 It's a way we have at old Yale, sir, It's a way we have at old Yale, sir, It's a way we have at old Yale, sir, To drive dull care a-way,.... To drive dull care a-way,.... To drive dull care a-way.....

2 For we think it is no sin, sir, To take the Freshmen in, sir, And ease them of their tin, sir, To drive dull care a-way,.... To drive dull care a-way..... To drive dull care a-way.....

3 For we think it is but right, sir,
On Wednesday and Saturday night, sir,
To get most gloriously tight, sir,
To drive dull care away.   Cho.

4 Brother Quidam is up in a pear tree,
Brother Quidam is up in a pear tree,
Brother Quidam is up in a pear tree,
Io! Io! Io!
  Cho. Io! Io! Io! Io! Io! Io!
  Once so merrily drinks he,

Twice so merrily drinks he,
Thrice so merrily drinks he,
Io! Io! Io!

5 Brother Quidam's a jolly good fellow.
Brother Quidam's a jolly good fellow,
Brother Quidam's a jolly good fellow,
As all of us can say.
  Cho. As all of us can say,
  As all of us can say.
  Once so merrily, etc.

Oh! does the Freshmen smoke, Oh! does the Freshmen smoke, Oh! does the lathery
Oh! no, it makes him sick, Oh! no, it makes him sick, Oh! no, it makes him

Freshmen smoke, Ça, Ça, lath - ery smoke, Oh! does the Fresh-men smoke?
lath - ery sick. Ça, Ça, lath - ery sick, Oh! no, it makes him sick.

"LATHERY."

Air.—*Was kommt der über das Höh'.*

1 What cometh there from the hills,
What cometh there from the hills,
What cometh there from the lathery hills,
Ça, Ça, lathery hills,
What cometh there from the hills?

2 There cometh a tutor grim, etc.

3 What bringeth he in his hand, etc.
4 He bringeth a condition, etc.
5 He bringeth it not for me. etc.

BIENNIALS.

Tune.—*Old Hundred.*

Biennials are a bore—ore—ore—ǀ
Biennials are a bore—ore—ore—

SAW MY LEG OFF.

Saw my leg off, saw my leg off, saw my leg off, short.

Saw my leg off, saw my leg off, saw my leg off, short.

B-A-BA.

Chorus in unison.

1 B - a - ba, b - e - be, b - i - bi, ba, be; bi, b - o - bo, ba-be-bi-bo; b - u-bu, ba-be-bi-bo-bu.
2 C - a - ca, c - e - ce, etc.
3 D - a - da, d - e - de, etc.
4 F - a - fa, f - e - fe, and so on.

Allegro giocoso.

1. Van Amburgh is the man, who goes to all the shows, He goes in - to the li - on's den, and tells you all he knows; He sticks his head in - to the li - on's mouth, And keeps it there a - while,, And when he takes it out a - gain, he greets you with a smile.

CHORUS

_ff_ The el - e - phant now goes round, the band be-gins to play, The boys around the monkey's cage, Had better keep a - way.

2 First comes the African Polar Bear, oft called the Iceberg's daughter,
She's been known to eat three tubs of ice, then call for soda water ;
She wades in the water up to her knees, not fearing any harm,
And you may grumble all you please, and she don't care a "darn."— _Chorus_

3 That Hyena in the next cage, most wonderful to relate,
Got awful hungry the other day, and ate up his female mate ;
He's a very ferocious beast, don't go near him, little boys,
For when he's mad he shakes his tail, and makes this awful noise. _Imitation of growling.—Chorus_

4 Next comes the Anaconda Boa Constrictor, oft called Anaconda for brevity,
He's noted the world throughout for his age and great longevity ;
He can swallow himself, crawl through himself, and come out again with facility,
He can tie himself up in a double-bow-knot with his tail, and wink with the greatest agility.—_Chorus._

5 Next comes the Vulture, awful bird, from the mountain's highest tops,
He's been known to eat up little girls, and then to lick his chops ;
Oh, the show it can't go on, there's too much noise and confusion,
Oh ladies stop, feeding those monkeys peanuts, it'll injure their constitution.—_Chorus._

AIR.—"BATTLE CRY OF FREEDOM."

1 Mary had a little lamb, its fleece was white as snow. Shouting the bat-tle cry of freedom. And everywhere that Mary went the lamb was sure to go. Shouting the bat-tle cry of free-dom,

The Union forev-er! Hurrah, boys, hurrah! Down with the traitor, and up with the star, And everywhere that Mary went the lamb was sure to go. Shout-ing the bat-tle cry of free-dom,

2 It followed her to school one day, which was against the rule, *Chorus.*
For it made the children laugh and play to see a lamb at shool. *Chorus.*

3 And so the teacher turned him out, but still he lingered near. *Chorus.*
And waited patiently about till Mary did appear. *Cho.*

4 " What makes the lamb love Mary so?" the children all did cry, *Chorus.*
" 'Cause Mary loves the lamb, you know," the teacher did reply. *Cho.*

* The third line of the chorus should be a repetition of the second line of the verse immediately preceding.

THE SHEEPSKIN.

1. When first I saw a "Sheepskin," In Prex's hand I spied it. I'd

given my hat and boots, I would, If I could have been beside it ; But now that last Biennial's past: I

"skinned" and "fizzled" through ; And so, in spite of scrapes and flunks, *I'll* have a sheepskin too.

CHORUS.

I'll have a sheepskin too, I'll have a sheepskin too , The race is run, the Prize is won, I'll have a sheepskin too.

I'll have a sheepskin too, I'll have a sheepskin too ; The race is run, the Prize is won, I'll have a sheepskin too.

2 Green elms are waving o'er us,
Green grass beneath our feet,
The ring is round, and on the ground
We sit a class complete ;
But when these elms shall shed their leaves,
This grass be turned to hay,
The noble class of Fifty-four,
Will all be far away.
We'll be Alumni too,
We'll be Alumni too,
With white degrees we'll take our ease,
And be Alumni too.

3 I tell you what, my classmates,
My mind it is made up,
I'm coming back three years from this,
To take that silver cup ;
I'll bring along the "*requisite*,"
A little white-haired lad,
With "bib" and fixings all complete,
And I shall be his "dad."
And I shall be his dad,
And I shall be his dad,
And you shall see how this "A. B."
Will look when he's a dad.

4 Then swell the chorus louder,
And make the old elms ring ;
Remember, fellows, one and all,
This is our parting "sing,"
And blow the smoke and music out,
In volume full and strong,
Till old "Grove Hall," "York Square,"
and all
Shall hear our farewell song.
Shall hear our farewell song,
Shall hear our farewell song,
Till old "Grove Hall," "York Square,"
and all
Shall hear our farewell song.

5 This lemonade it has no "stick,"
But let us take a glass,
And fill us up a "stirrup cup,"
Together as a class ;
And then before we say farewell,
And part to meet no more,
Drink to the Sophomore "Martyrs"
Of the class of Fifty-four.
The class of Fifty-four,
The class of Fifty-four,
A long adieu, oh, tried and true,
Old class of Fifty-four.

WOODEN-SPOON SONG.

BY A. L. EDWARDS, '57.

AIR— "*A little more Cider.*"

1 Old Yale holds many honors
In reach of every son,
And scarce a son departs from her,
Without some honor won ;
While hundreds take these honors,
'Twixt every twelfth full moon,
But one a year and only one,
Can take the "Wooden Spoon."

Chorus—Then take the Wooden Spoon,
Oh ! take the Wooden Spoon,
Of all the honors Yale affords,
Oh take the Wooden Spoon.

2 When first we enter College,
With prospects bright and fair
Appointments are the corner-stones
Of castles in the air ;
But when we find their *price a song*,
And do not like the tune,
We feel that it is better far,
To take the "Wooden Spoon."

Chorus—Then take, &c.

3 There's not a land whose morning sun
O'er College walls arises,
That cannot boast as well as we
Of premiums and prizes ;
But where's the man in this broad world,
Save Yale's own jolly "Jun',"
Whose high ambition ever thought
To take the "Wooden Spoon."

Chorus—Then take, &c.

4 When College life has passed away,
And battle-life's begun,
This Wooden Spoon will ever be
A type of College fun ;
But soon you'll choose your better half,
You'll be a *fraction* soon,
And *fractions of a fraction* then,
May use this "Wooden Spoon."

Chorus—Then take the Wooden Spoon,
Oh ! take the Wooden Spoon,
Of all the honors Yale affords,
Oh take the Wooden Spoon.

SO SAY WE. Air—America.

So say we all of us, So say we all of us, So say we all; So say we
all of us, So say we all of us, So say we all of us, So say we all.

RE-UNION SONG.

CLASS OF '56.

Air—"America"

1 Once more united here,
  'Mid scenes we all hold dear,
    Greet we our Class—
  In all our scattered homes
  Low cots and lofty domes—
  Where'er a classmate roams,
    God bless our Class.

2 Health to our absent ones —
  Whom busy memory runs
    Glad to recall—
  Where'er in distant lands
  This night a brother stands,
  Clasping his unpressed hands,—
    God bless them all.

3 Old friends here greet us yet,
  But friends we'll ne'er forget,
    Rest cold and pale.

Oh! while our songs ascend
Must strains of sadness blend
And mournful mem'ries tend,
  To graves of Yale,

4 Our Alma Master! thee
  Peace and prosperity,
    Shall never fail.
  Memory shall linger long
  These charmed scenes among,
  And oft inspire the song—
    God save Old Yale!

ANTIOCH.

Maestoso.   Presto

ff 1. There was a man in our town, And he was won-drous wise, He jumped in-to a
   2. And when he saw his eyes were out, With all his might and main, He jumped in-to an-

bram - ble bush, He jumped in - to a bram - ble bush, And scratched out both his
oth - er bush, He jumped in - to an - oth - er bush, And scratched them in a -

eyes, And scratched out both his eyes, And scratched, and scratched out both his eyes.
gain, And scratched them in a - gain, And scratched, and scratched them in a - gain.

And scratched out both his eyes, And scratched out both his eyes,

DERBY RAM.

CLASS OF '54.

f 1. I came an Em-erald Fresh-man, With just a do-zen shirts, A

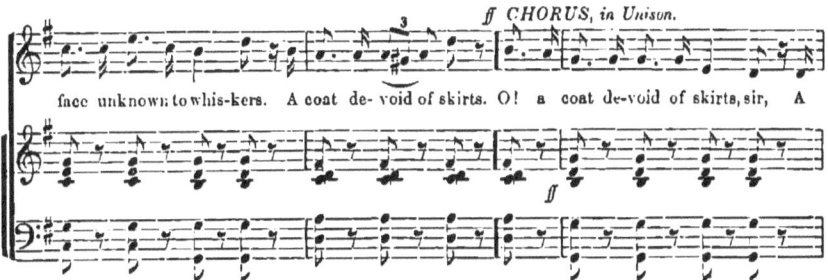

face unknown to whis-kers. A coat de-void of skirts. O! a coat de-void of skirts, sir, A

coat devoid of skirts, O! a coat devoid of skirts, sir, A coat de-void of skirts.

2 On knowledge was I bent, sir,
    For learning I did pant,
So, to College I was sent, sir,
    To see the Elephant.
      O ! to see, &c.

3 The animal is "some," sir,
    I've scrutinized him through,
From trunk to tip of tail, sir,
    I rather think I'll do.
      O ! I rather, &c.

4 O ! College is the place, sir,
    For jollity and fun ;

For four years take your ease, sir,
    Repent when you have done.
      O ! repent, &c.

5 But now old Yale, I leave her,
    To breast the waves of life,
I'm going to serve my country,
    And sport a pretty wife.
      O ! and sport, &c.

6 When I get into business,
    And count my numerous boys,
I'll send them to old Yale, sir,
    To taste to her bunkum joys.
      O ! to taste, &c.

THE BLACK BRIGADE.

Words and Music by DAN. D. EMMET. By permission.

We're de Brack Brigade, Why don't ye let her rip? Jeemeses Ribber Massa Greely, O!

2 We am the snolly-gosters, (*Repeat.*)
An' lubs Jim Ribber oysters.
Cho. Den harness up, etc.

3 We're gwine to fight de South, O, (*Repeat.*)
All by de 'word ob mouth', O.
Cho. Den harness up, etc.

4 To fight for death an' glory, (*Repeat.*)
Am quite annudder story. *Cho.*

5 Old John Brown dey strung 'im, (*Repeat.*)
As high as Haman hung 'im. *Cho.*

6 I'll take my boat an' paddle, (*Repeat.*)
For freedom will skydaddle. *Cho.*

PRESENTATION-DAY SONG.

Air.—"WHERE, OH, WHERE ARE THE HEBREW CHILDREN?"

CLASS OF '53.

Allegretto.

1, U - bi sunt Bienni - a - les char - tæ, U - bi sunt Bien-ni - a - les char - tæ,
Pro - fes - sor - i - bus pa - bu - lo e - runt, Pro - fes - sor - i - bus pa - bu - lo e - runt.

Om - nes a no - bis pro - stra - tæ? (Fie - ri non po - test quin.)
Pro - fes - sor - i - bus pa - bu - lo e - runt, Non alia re dig - næ sunt.

3 Ubi est meus parvus equus   *Bis.*
Qui de me est bene meritus?
(Per quem stabat, quominus——)
Actum est de meo equo,   *Ter.*
Ex equo sic pugnavi.

8 Ubi sunt hi professores   *Bis.*
Quibus modo cœnam dedimus?
(Qui nihil prætermiserunt quin——)
Laborant stomacho, sed nihil interest, *Ter.*
Si sheepskin valet, bene est,

4 Ubi classes inferiores?   *Bis.*
Invidentes hic a tergo:
Macte, pueri, virtute!

Non cujusvis est æquare   *Ter.*
Classem quinquaginta tres!

5 Ubi sunt Seniores ante nos?   *Bis.*
Haud scio an terra marique
Ubique dispersi sint
Iidem sunt qui semper fuerunt; *Ter.*
Ex civitate pulsi sunt.

6 Ubi est Gulielmus Wickham   *Bis.*
Qui sæculare carmen cantat?
Vermes habent corpus id.
Alios centum annos abhinc,   *Ter.*
Vermes devorarint nos.

2 Now Peter Gray he fell in love, all with a nice young girl,
The first three letters of her name were L - U - C, Anna Quirl. *Cho.*

3 But just as they were going to wed, her papa he said "No,"
And consequently she was sent way off to Ohio. *Cho.*

4 And Peter Gray he went to trade for furs and other skins,
Till he was caught and scalp - y - ed by the bloody Iudians. *Cho.*

5 When Lucy Anna heard the news, she straightway took to bed,
And never did get up again until she di - i - ed. *Cho.*

Air.—"LANDLORD, FILL THE FLOWING BOWL."

Allegretto.

f 1. Landlord, fill the flow-ing bowl, Un - til it doth run o - - ver,

Land-lord, fill the flow-ing bowl, Un - til it doth run o - ver.

CHORUS.

ff For to-night we'll mer-ry, mer-ry be, For to-night we'll merry, merry be,

For to-night we'll merry, merry be, To mor - row we'll get so - ber.

2 The man that drinks good whiskey punch,
And goes to bed right mellow,
Lives as he ought to live,
And dies a jolly good fellow. *Cho.*

3 The man who drinks cold water pure,
And goes to bed quite sober,

Falls as the leaves do fall,
So early in October. *Cho.*

4 But he who drinks just what he likes
And getteth "half-seas over,"
Will live until he dies, perhaps,
And then lie down in clover. *Cho.*

SOLO. *Andante*

1. On Springfield mountain there did dwell A nice young man, I knew him well I - ell, sing

CHORUS.

Tu - ri - lu - ri - tu - ri - lay, Sing tu - ri - lu - ri - tu - ri - lay - i - a.

2 On Monday morning he did go
   Down to the meadow for to mow. etc.

3 He scarce had mowed half round the field,
   When a pesky sarpent bit his heel. *Cho.*

4 He raised his scythe and struck a blow,
   Which laid the pesky sarpent low. *Cho.*

5 He took the sarpent in his hand,
   And posted off to Molly Brand. *Cho.*

6 "Oh, Johnny dear, why did you go
   Down to the meadow for to mow? *Cho.*

7 "Oh, Molly dear, I thought you knowed
   'Twas father's field and must be mowed. *Cho.*

8 Now this young man gave up the ghost
   And did to Abraham's bosom post. *Cho.*

9 And thus he cried as up he went,
   "Oh, pesky, cruel, sar - pi - ent." *Cho.*

10 Now all young men, a warning take,
   Beware of the bite of a great big snake. *Cho.*

AH ME!

47

By G. L. Bishop '66.

Adagio mosso.

1. Tolling soft-ly, slowly, now, The old bell ring-eth out its mourn, Tolling soft-ly, sad-ly,

now That Six-ty Six, a-las! is gone. Ah we! that now must part Ah we! that now must

part, That now must leave old scenes and tricks, In part-ing with our Six-ty-Six.

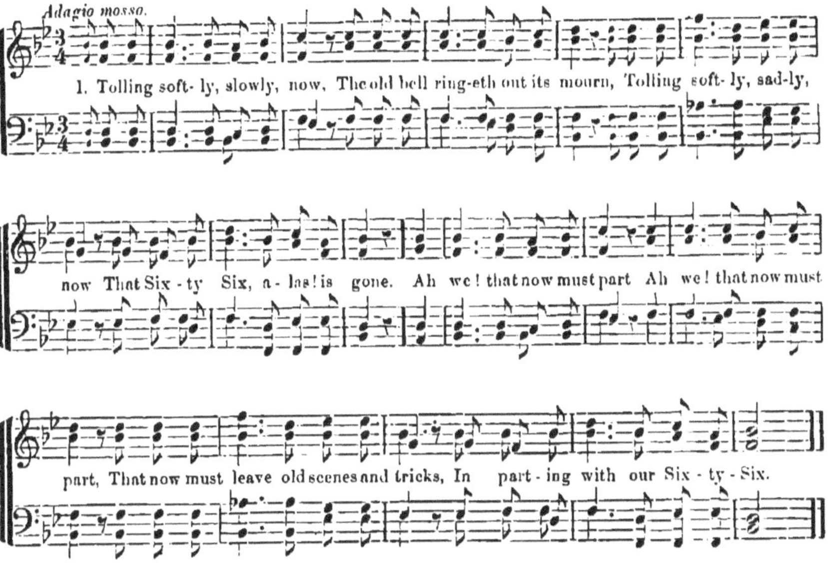

2 Waving softly, very slow,
  Each old tree waveth us good-bye,
Waving songs of years ago,
That now in memory treasured lie.
*Chorus.—*Ah we! &c.

3 Tolling softly, a sad song
  The old bell endeth with a cry
Tolling sadly, lingering long,
As we bid each one good-bye.
*Chorus.—*Ah we! &c.

GOOD NIGHT.

Sostenuto.

p 1. Good night, ladies! Good night, ladies! Good night, ladies! We're going to leave you now.

Allegro.   *Repeat pp*

f Merri-ly we roll along, roll a-long, roll a-long, Merrily we roll along, o'er the dark, blue sea.

2 Farewell, ladies, etc.

3 Sweet dreams, ladies, etc.

THE OLD MOUNTAIN TREE.

JAMES G. CLARK. By permission.

1 Oh! the home we loved by the bounding deep, Where the hills in glo-ry stood; And the moss-grown graves where our fath-ers sleep, 'Neath the boughs of the wav-ing wood; We re-mem-ber yet with a fond re-gret For the rock and the flow-'ry lea, Where we once used to play thro' the

long, long day In the shade of the old mountain tree, In the shade of the old mountain tree.

2 We are pilgrims now in a stranger land,
And the joys of youth are passed;
Kind friends are gone, but the old tree stands
Unharm'd by the warring blast;
Oh, may the lark sing in the clouds of spring,
And the swan on the silver sea,
But we mourn for the shade where the wild bird made
Her nest in the old mountain tree,
Her nest in the old mountain tree.

3 Oh! the time went by like a tale that's told
In a land of song and mirth,
And many a form in the church-yard cold,
Finds rest from the cares of earth ;
And many a day will wander away,
O'er the waves of the western sea,
And the heart will pine, and vainly pray
For a grave by the old mountain tree,
For a grave by the old mountain tree.

THREE CROWS.

It is the custom for some one to "line" each stanza before it is sung.

f 1. There were three crows sat on a tree, And they were black as crows could be.

2 Said one old crow unto his mate,
"What shall we do for grub to eat?"

3 "There lies a horse on yonder plain
Who's by some cruel butcher slain."

4 "We'll perch upon his bare back-bone,
And pick his eyes out one by one."

1 Those eve - ning bells, those eve-ning bells, How many a tale their mu-sic tells, Of

youth and home, and that sweet time, When last I heard their sooth-ing chime, Those

eve - ning bells, those even - ing bells, How many a tale their mu - sic tells.

2 Those joyous hours are passed away,
And many a heart that then was gay,
Within the tomb now darkly dwells,
And hears no more those evening bells.
     Those evening, &c.

3 And so 'twill be when I am gone,
That tuneful peal will still ring on,
While other bards shall walk these dells
And sing your praise, sweet evening bells.
     Those evening, &c.

PARTING SONG.

Air—"*Evening Bells.*"

BY EDWARD M. WRIGHT '65.

1 Four revolutions of the sun
We've numbered slowly, one by one,
In which we've climbed those lights sublime,
Where dwelt the Bards of long past time,
And sung those songs, and learned that lore,
Which we shall sing and know no more.

2 Oft cheered by Fancy's gorgeous ray,
We've panted for this closing day ;
But not as every throbbing heart
Feels that the hour has come to part,
Oppressed with thoughts we ne'er can tell,
We sadly murmur our farewell.

3 And when again the shadows fall,
Enveloping each gray old hall,
Then others 'neath these Elms will meet,
These walks be pressed by other feet,
And all that we can claim at last,
Will be the echoes of the past.

4 And now we leave this resting place,
With loins girt up for life's long race ;
And, Brothers, when that race is o'er,
Then may we meet to part no more,
But safe within that Better Land,
Continue an unbroken band.

PARTING SONG.

BY S. W. DUFFIELD, '63.

Air—"*Evening Bells.*"

1 The sadness of each vanished year
Falls on us as we linger here,
And thoughts of moments past arise
To pain our hearts and dim our eyes,
For these broad Elms no more shall see
Our long united '63.

2 To some the East shall open wide
The treasure of her wealth and pride,—
To some the West with lavish hand
Shall grant the fairest of her land,
And so shall part, by land and sea,
Our long united '63.

3 To some the sound of war shall come,
The shrill-toned fife, the rolling drum,
And far from those they love the best
Shall be, perchance, their latest rest ;
And so shall part, where'er they be,
Our long united '63,

4 But yet the moments still delay,
These moments of our final day,
And so we lay aside again
All thoughts of care which cause us pain,
Until the parting comes, and we
Shall leave old Yale with '63.

BIENNIAL-JUBILEE SONG.

BY W. E. BLISS, '67.

Air—"*Evening Bells*"

1 Alumni Hall ! Alumni Hall !
Ere we had passed Biennial,
Thy dreaded walls we shunned through fear,
Nor would we near thy doors appear,
But now examination's o'er
Our cares and fears exist no more.

2 Our cramming past, our labor done,
Our goal and crown of victory won,
With naught to mar this happy hour,
And freed from every tutor's power,
Here have we come, with joy and glee,
To celebrate our Jubilee.

3 Biennial's past : Biennial's past,
And Junior year has come at last,
Its days will quickly pass along,
'Mid joy and mirth, 'mid cheer and song.
Then let its first glad welcome be
This, our Biennial Jubilee.

JOHN BROWN.

John Brown had a little injun,
John Brown had a little injun,
John Brown had a little injun,
One little injun boy.
One little, two little, three little injun,
Four little, five little, six little injun,
Seven little, eight little, nine little injun,
Ten little injun boys.
Ten little, nine little, eight little injun,
Seven little, six little, five little injun,
Four little, three little, two little injun,
One little injun boy.

1. Hail to thee, queen of the si - lent night, Shine clear, shine bright, yield thy pensive light;

Blithe-ly we'll dance in thy sil - ver ray. Hap-pi - ly passing the hours a - way.

Must we not love the stil - ly night, Dressed in her robes of blue and white? Heaven's arches ring,

Stars wink and sing, Hail, silent night.   Fairy moonlight   Fai-ry, fai-ry, fai-ry moon-

Fairy moonlight.

Stars wink and sing, Hail, silent night   Fairy moonlight, Fairy moon - - -

light   Fai-ry moonlight Fairy moonlight   Fai - ry, fai - ry, fai - ry moonlight.

Fai-ry moonlight. Fairy moon - - - - - light.

2.

Dart thy pure beams from thy throne on high,
Beam on through sky, robed in azure dye ;
We'll laugh and we'll sport while the night-bird sings,
Flapping the dew from his sable wings,
Sprites love to sport in the still moonlight,
Play with the pearls of shadowy night ;
    Then let us sing,
    Time's on the wing,
    Hail, silent night,
    Fairy moonlight.

IVY SONG.

Words by JAMES BRAND, 56.

TENOR.

1. Symbol of our trust ! When sorrow Darkens on our shad - owy way.

ALTO.

AIR.

1. Symbol of our trust ! When sorrow Darkens on our shad - owy way.

BASS.

Be thou sign of bright to - morrow, Climb to where the sunbeams play.

Be thou sign of bright to - morrow, Climb to where the sunbeams play.

2 Be thou mightier to inspire,
　　Truer than the sculptured bust;
And while clinging, climbing, higher,
　　Tell that we are more than dust.

3 Symbol, too, of patient waiting,
　　Waiting for the tardy years,
Torn by storms, but still creating
　　Leaves of hope and charms for tears;—

4 Planted thus by Friendship's fingers,
　　Silently to strengthen there.
Seal the thought that round thee lingers,
　　Witness our last, saddest prayer.

5 Frail memento ! softly waking
　　Memories set in checkered light,
Of our meeting and our breaking,
　　Thee we leave to God and Night.

G. F. ROOT.

SONG OF THE SPOON.

Words by R. E. Smythe, '66.

Music by Otto.

1 Eyes of beau-ty, throng'd around thee Gaze up-on thee, Spoon, to night, Up-i-dee.
In thy presence all our hearts Are full of mer-ry, made de-light, Up-i-dee,

Up-i-dee, Up-i-dee, Up-i-dee, Up-i-da. Laugh, be merry

mer-ry, mer-ry June; Kind, be-nig nant June; jol-ly, jol-ly June; To her children

gives the no-ble, gives the no-ble Wood-en Spoon.

To her children gives the no-ble, no-ble Wooden

Blessings ev-er be up-on thee, on thy hon-est wood-en face, Strangely carv-en,

mystic meanings Shadow from thy state-ly grace, Up-i-dee, Up-i-dee, Up-i-dee, Up-i-da

2d time omit to Coda.

While the wave shocks Mad - ly the rocks. Drops fall in spray, Jew - els are they

In the robes of night, In the locks of storms, Making darkness bright, Lighting our way.

Then the dark, fear - ful wave, Sailors' home, sail-ors' grave, Seems to glow with de-light,

And it shines in pleas - ant mem'ries Through the night... Thus thro' our days

When the waves beat high, And our souls re - ply In one constant tune, Still shall it cheer,

Repeat with same words.   D. C al 𝄋 e poi la Coda

Looking back upon mem'ries held so dear, Wreathing the spoon. Spoon, Spoon, Spoon, Spoon.

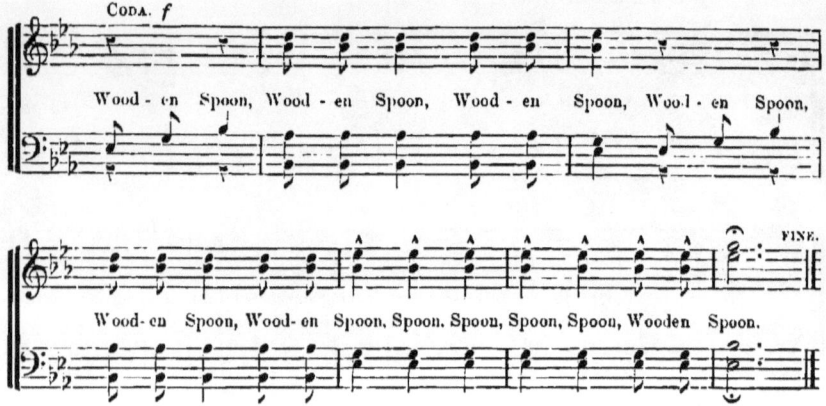

Wood - en Spoon, Wood - en Spoon, Wood - en Spoon, Wood - en Spoon,

Wood- en Spoon, Wood- en Spoon, Spoon, Spoon, Spoon, Spoon, Wooden Spoon.

But another year together,
And with faces sad and pale,
Upidee, upidee, etc.
We must leave thee, and whatever
We have had most dear at Yale.
Upidee, upidee, etc.
Other voices merrily will sing
Thee a very king,
Till the startled moon
Yields her homage to the noble Wooden Spoon.
Through the ages, ever dearer,
Shall thy glory move along,
And forever, louder, clearer,
Shall thy praises swell the song.

2 Scatter flowers, scatter laughter,
In his path who bears the Spoon;
Upidee, upidee, etc.
And around him ever after,
Still shall ring the merry tune.
Upidee, upidee, etc.
Smile upon him, fairest of the fair;
Let your beauty rare
Grace the peerless boon;
Brightest, dearest, noblest treasure, Wooden Spoon.
And an honor shall it ever
Be to him, the highest, best,
'Till our college bond shall sever,
And the parting hand be pressed.

WOODEN SPOON SONG.

BY P. R. PORTER, '67.

AIR.—" *Song of the Spoon.*"

1 Welcome, welcome, eve of gladness,
Hail, O hour of joy supreme!
All ye golden lamps of heaven
Now with softest influence beam.
In your beauty kindly smile on us,

Bright-eyed Hesperus,
Silver-throned Moon,
While we hold the mystic revels of the Spoon.
Shout the chorus ever joyful:
Welcome, Mirth and Revelry,
Welcome, Beauty, Song, and Friendship;
Hail, O Prince of Jollity!

Come rosy hours
And ye sweet powers:
All ye blithe gnomes,
Where'er each roams;
Nymphs divinely fair,
Forms of earth or air,
Sylphs and houris rare,
From your bright homes
Hither come on swift wing,
And the Spoon homage bring.

To his high festival
All ye Fairies, Loves, and Graces,
He doth call.
Come Titania, queen,
And fair Mab serene,
From the silver sheen
Of the full orb'd moon;
While eyes as bright
And forms as light,
Gathered here to night,
Welcome the Spoon.

3 Many an hour of festal gladness
We have known together here:
None of pleasure so unmingled—
Brightest of the golden year.
Where, O where are hearts so light and free!
Then who would not be,
Be a jolly June
Shouting glory to the good old Wooden Spoon!
Heart to heart swells in the chorus;
Let it thunder forth to thee:
Live forever, sung and honored,
Peerless Prince of Jollity.

THE WOODEN SPOON.

THE WOODEN SPOON.

BY A. E. KENT, '54.

AIR— "*Benny Havens O.*"

1 Come all ye jolly Juniors, and stand up in a
row,
For singing sentimentally we're going for to
go,
We care not for appointments, for morning
night or noon,
We're singing loud the praises of the jolly
Wooden Spoon,
The jolly Wooden Spoon!
The jolly Wooden Spoon!
We're singing loud the praises of the jolly
Wooden Spoon!

2 To the fearful Freshmen we would sing,
who sit so far behind,—
Oh! dare not gaze upon the spoon lest you
be stricken blind!
Look forward for a year or so, you will be
Soph'mores soon,
And Sophomore Biennial decides the Wooden
Spoon,
Decides the Wooden Spoon, &c.

3 What adds to our enjoyment, our pride and
glory too,
Is that so many ladies fair are present to our
view,
We thank them for their favor,—it is a
mighty boon :
We sing as well their praises as the glories
of the Spoon!
The glories of the Spoon, &c.

4 But one short year remains to us and we'll
be here no more,
So if you think of husbands from the Class
of Fifty-Four,
You must, sweet ladies, be on hand, you
cannot be too soon ;
Permit us to propose to you the man who
has the Spoon!
The man who has the Spoon, &c.

5 And Sophomores, remember well, on you
our mantle falls—
'Tis yours to stand, in fifty-four, within
these hallowed walls!
Among you, though you know him not,
there stands an embryo June,
Whose name, upon the Tutor's books, is
writ against the Spoon!

6 Oh! now you Greek Oration man, we see
your curious look!
And those two Philosophicals with jealousy
are strook ;
For cochleaureati but join in this our tune,
And raise on high the glories of the jolly
Wooden Spoon!
The jolly Wooden Spoon, &c.

———

THE WOODEN SPOON.

AUTHOR UNKNOWN.

AIR—"*Auld Lang Syne.*"

1 When first the Fresh to College hies,
His leisure time to spend,
He wears away his sleepless eyes,
High scholarship his end ;
But soon he finds that few attain
That much desired boon,
And with all effort seeks to gain
The far-famed Wooden Spoon.
Then loudly sing, each son of Yale,
This worthy, honor'd boon,
He who attempts will rarely fail
To gain the wooden spoon.

2 When in his chamber lone and drear,
He wastes the midnight oil,
He fears not, nor has cause to fear
That he shall lose his toil,
For visions bright flit round his head,
And Hope, appearing soon,
High o'er the curtains of his bed
Display the *Wooden Spoon*.

3 'Tis this supports him when despair
Else would oppress him sore ;
'Tis this which drives away his care,
And bids him fear no more.
When Horace frets and Euclid bores
Each luckless tutored loon—
He, o'er his lesson dreaming, snores,
And views the Wooden Spoon.

4 And when appointments do appear,
He can exulting say
With gladsome heart I now may cheer
O'er my success to-day.
I once to Yale a *Fresh* did come,
But now a jolly *Jun*',
Returning to my distant home,
I bear the Wooden Spoon.

OFT IN OUR FUTURE COURSE.

A PARTING SONG.

AIR.—"OFT IN THE STILLY NIGHT."

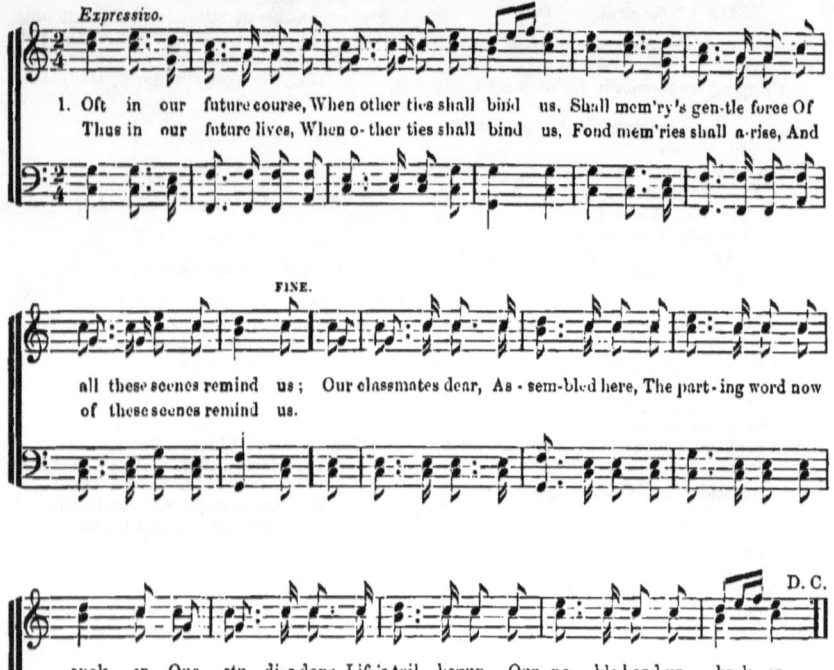

1. Oft in our future course, When other ties shall bind us, Shall mem'ry's gen-tle force Of
   Thus in our future lives, When o-ther ties shall bind us, Fond mem'ries shall a-rise, And

all these scenes remind us; Our classmates dear, As-sem-bled here, The part-ing word now
of these scenes remind us.

spok-en, Our stu-dies done, Life's toil begun,—Our no-ble band un-brok-en.

2 When we remember those
  Young hearts with ours united,
Who, ere our journey's close,
  In bloom of youth were blighted;
    We'll drop a tear
    Upon their bier,
While fondly we will cherish
    Their blooming youth,
    Their spotless truth,
Nor let their memories perish.
Thus we'll remember those
  Young hearts with ours united,
Who, ere our journey's close,
  In bloom of youth were blighted.

3 Then oft in future years,
  When other ties shall bind us,
With mingled smiles and tears
  We'll of these scenes remind us.
    Our classmates dear,
    Who with us here
Have trod life's path together,
    And in our heart
    Shall e'er have part,
And be forgotten never.
Thus oft in future years,
  When other ties shall bind us,
With mingled smiles and tears
  We'll of these scenes remind us.

BROTHERS' CAMPAIGN SONG.

AIR.—"PIRATE'S CHORUS."

By G. C. S. SOUTHWORTH, '63.

2 Gentle and sacred covenant tie,
Binding our hearts for aye,
Altars above
Waft their incense of love,
On soft pinions of pleasure,
Wherever we may rove,—Shout !—*Chorus.* Ever, etc.

3 Pledged by this altar our holiest shrine,
Girded with love divine,
Pealing our cry,
Of the battle, on high,
On, onward press proudly,
To conquer or die,—Shout !—*Chorus.* Ever, etc.

1ST TENOR.

1. In heav'n, in heav'n the rapt'rous song be - gan, And sweet, and sweet se - raphic fire, Thro'

2ND TENOR.

1ST BASS.

5 With joy, with joy the cho- rus we'll re - peat, Glo- ry, glo- ry to God in heav'n, Good

2ND BASS.

all thro' all the shin-ing le- gions ran, Thro' all the shin-ing le- gions ran, And

will and peace are now, are now complete, Good will and peace are now complete, Christ

strung and tun'd the lyre, And strung and tun'd the lyre, And strung and tun'd the lyre. *D. C.*

to the earth is giv'n. Christ to the earth is giv'n, Christ to the earth is giv'n. *D. C.*

2. Swift thro' the vast ex-panse it flew, it flew, And loud, loud the ech-o roll'd. And

6. Hail, Prince of peace, for-ev - er

loud the ech-o roll'd. And loud the ech-o roll'd the ech-o

hail, for-ev - er hail, The Sa - - - viour of man-kind. The Saviour

And angels flew with ea - ger joy, And an-gels flew with ea - ger joy, To

And angels flew with ea-ger joy, And an-gels flew with ea - ger joy, To

bring the news to man To bring the news to man, And

bring the news to man To bring the news to man, And

angels flew with ea - ger joy, To bring the news to man, the news to

angels flew with ea - ger joy, To bring the news to man. the news to

Hark! the che - ru - bic ar - mies shout, And glo - ry leads the song,.... And

And glo - ry leads the song,.... And

glo - ry leads the song, Hark! hark! the Cherubic armies shout, And glory leads the song, And

glo - ry leads the song, Hark! hark! the Cherubic armies shout, And glory leads the song, And

glo - ry leads the song, And glo-ry leads the song, Good will and peace are heard thro'out th'har-

glo - ry leads the song, And glo-ry leads the song, Good will and peace are heard thro'out th'har-

- mo - nious heav'n-ly throng, Good will and peace are heard thro'out th'har-

. mo - nious heav'n-ly throng, Good will and peace are heard thro'out th'har-

- monious heav'nly throng, Good will and peace are heard thro'out th'harmonious heav'nly throng.

- monious heav'nly throng, Good will and peace are heard thro'out th'harmonious heav'nly throng.

[A SERENADE.]

Dolce. _p_ 1 Stars of the sum - mer night, Far in you a - zure deeps, Hide, hide your

_p_ 2 Moon of the sum - mer night, Far down yon west - ern steeps, Sink, sink in

gold-en light, She sleeps,—my lady sleeps, She sleeps, she sleeps,—my la - dy sleeps.

sil - ver light, She sleeps,—my lady sleeps, She sleeps, she sleeps,—my la - dy sleeps.

3 Wind of the summer night,
  Where yonder woodbine creeps,
Fold, fold thy pinions light,
  She sleeps, my lady sleeps.

4 Dreams of the summer night,
  Tell her, her lover keeps
Watch, while in slumbers light
  She sleeps, my lady sleeps.

PARTING HYMN.

CHORUS. *Andante espressivo.*

In part from MENDELSSOHN.

1st and 2d Tenor. *rp* *cres.*

p 1. Lamb of God, behold us meet-ing Here, up-on thy ho-ly day, Bless us in the moments fleeting, While within thy courts we stay, While within thy courts we stay.

1st Bass. *cres.*

3. When the day of life is fa-ding Fast in-to its ev-'ning grey, Join us where no more in-vad-ing Fears or doubts can lead astray, Fears or doubts can lead a-stray.

Soli.

Bless us parting, Bless us start-ing Out up-on life's weary way, Bless us part-ing, Bless us start-ing Out up-on life's weary way, Bless us part-ing, Bless us start-ing Out up-

Where death nev-er-more can sev-er Chains of love that bind to-day, Where death nev-er-more can sev-er Chains of love that bind to-day, Where death nev-er-more can sev-er Chains of

rit. *f* Tutti. Tutti. *A tempo.*

on life's weary way. 2. Brightest joys are soonest ended; Parting scenes to all must come;

love that bind to-day.

Pleasure is with sor-row blend ed; Friends must from each other roam. May thy

guid-ing grace a - bid-ing Lead to rest in heav'n, to rest in heav'n, our

home, Lead to rest, lead to rest in heav'n...., our home.

AULD LANG SYNE.

1. Should auld ac-quaintance be for-got, And nev-er brot' to mind? Should

auld ac-quaintance be for-got, And days of auld lang syne? For

CHORUS.

days of auld lang syne, my dear, For auld lang syne, We'll

tak' a cup o' kind-ness yet, For auld lang syne.

2 We two have run about the braes,
    And pult the gowans fine;
  But we've wandered monie a weary foot,
    Sin' Auld Lang Syne—*Chorus.*

3 We two have paddled in the barn,
    Frae morning sun till dine;
  But seas between us braid have waved,
    Sin' Auld Lang Syne.—*Chorus*

ALUMNI SONG.

BY H. M. COLTON, '48.

AIR—"*Auld Lang Syne.*"

1 Should those old times be e'er forgot,
  So mellow and so hale;
Those good old times, those grand old times
  We passed at Yale;
When in youth's fiery blood, we felt
  So happy and so fine?
Come make your memories green again,
  For days o' lang syne;
    For days o' lang syne, my friends,
      For days o' lang syne;
    Come make your memories green again,
      For days o' lang syne.

2 We've come a host, each from his post,
  From pulpit and from bar;
From skillful tending of disease,
  And fields of war;
From hardy traffic on the land,
  And commerce on the brine;
To greet old Yale with kindness yet,
  For auld lang syne.
    For auld lang syne, my friends,
      For auld lang syne;
    To greet old Yale with kindness yet,
      For auld lang syne.

3 We all have wrought in mines of thought,
  And brought up various ore;
But many a mate has met his fate
  That sat with us of yore;
Should these old comrades be forgot
  Who thus do pale and pine?
We'll think of them with kindness yet,
  For days o' lang syne.
    For days o' lang syne, good friends,
      For days o' lang syne,
    We'll think of them with kindness yet,
      For days o' lang syne.

4 And we—frail remnant, large or small,
  Of bands that once were one;
We, too, must pass each in his place,
  Till all are gone.
Then there's a hand—let each one say—
  And gi' us a hand o' thine;
And we'll take a right good hearty shake,
  For auld lang syne.
    For auld lang syne, old mates,
      For auld lang syne;
    And we'll take a right good hearty shake
      For auld lang syne.

5 And though Time's frost be on our heads,
  And his cold within our bones;
And our heart's lone chambers echo not
  To other tones!
Yet ring we out in final shout
  This old and hearty line:
For th' oldest here is young enough,
  For auld lang syne;
    For auld lang syne, good sirs,
      For auld lang syne,
    For th' oldest here is young enough
      For auld lang syne.

PARTING SONG.

BY C. R. PALMER, '55.

AIR— "*Juvallera.*"

1 The day of departure has come, and
    our sail
  Already is spread to the favoring
    wind;
  Adieu, Alma Mater, Adieu, dear old
    Yale—
Bis. We leave you to-day when your sun
    has declined.
Chorus—Juvallera! Juvallera! Juvalle,
    valle, vallera, &c.

2 As sadly the last parting moments
    glide past,
  With thoughts of the years that have
    peacefully flown,
  We gaze upon life's stormy ocean at last,
Bis. And dread to embark on its waters
    alone
Chorus—Juvallera, &c.

3 Yet linger we may not, we sever to-day
  The last ties that fasten our bark to
    the shore;
  And through the wide waste take our
    wearisome way,
Bis. To meet ne'er again till the voyage
    be o'er.
Chorus—Juvallera, &c.

4 Then, comrades, as 'neath these dark
    trees we recline,
  We'll pledge one another to cherish
    this day,
  Around Fifty-five fondest memories
    shall turn,
Bis. And elm-girt old Yale be remembered
    for aye.
Chorus—Juvallera, &c.

PARTING ODE.

BY GEORGE PRATT, '57.

AIR— "*Auld Lang Syne.*"

1 Farewell! farewell! the parting word,
    To-day dissolves our band,
No more within these hallowed walls,
    Shall we united stand;
But e'er we part, pledge hand and heart,
    With truth that ne'er shall fail,
To swell the fame and glorious name,
    Of Fifty-seven and Yale.

2 Four summers bright, with sunny light,
    Have crowned the fleeting years,
Since first we met as strangers meet,
    With mingled hopes and fears;
But soon our hearts were bound in one,
    With friendship's golden chain,
Which, come what may in after years,
    Unsevered shall remain.

3 And though to distant homes we part,
    And enter earnest life,
The memory of our College days
    Will cheer us in the strife;
Like stars which shine through rifted clouds,
    And light the darkened heaven,
In after years sweet thoughts will come
    Of Yale and Fifty-seven.

4 Farewell! farewell! the parting word,
    To-day we sadly sing,
Though round our hearts the hopes of life,
    Like summer blossoms spring;
But let the years bring joy or tears,
    As youth and life decline,
"We'll take a cup of kindness yet,"
    For Yale and Auld Lang Syne!

PARTING ODE.

BY THERON BROWN, '56

AIR— "*Auld Lang Syne.*"

1 O! sad the light must fall to-night,
    And pensive blow the gale,
That lifts and swells, with fond farewells,
    The evening bells of Yale.

2 'Tis holy here! how deep and dear
    Resounds the long "good-bye;"
We ne'er shall shed a sweeter tear,
    Nor heave a purer sigh.

3 The daily themes, the passing schemes
    Our days of study knew,
Are nothing now but dying dreams:
    Adieu, my mates, adieu!

4 All, all are past, and soon the last
    Will fade from book and brain,
O! give and take, for memory's sake,
    The parting hand again!

5 Still in each breast, there burns, confessed,
    A longing to be FREE!
We gaze like eaglets from our nest
    And lift our wings to flee.

6 Away! for fame, the splendid star
    Of Fame, we, following, hail!
From home dismissed, no more to list
    The vesper bells of Yale.

PARTING SONG.

CLASS OF '56.

AIR— "*Auld Lang Syne.*"

1 Oh! sad and sweet the thoughts that throng
    Within our hearts to-night;
That mingle with our parting song
    As dawns the morning light.
Sweet thoughts of happy College years—
    Mem'ries that cannot die;
Sad thoughts,—too strong and deep for
    tears—
That stifle our "good-bye."

2 Sweet thoughts of days that rolled along,
    With brighter hopes and joys;
Sweet thoughts of days we spent among
    These elms as College boys.
Sad thoughts that, boys no longer now,
    We deal with life's stern cares;
Sad thoughts—that soon on every brow,
    Shall glisten silver hairs.

3 Sad thoughts that we, who, gathered here,
    Raise high this coral strain,
Must part—at best, for many a year—
    And may not meet again.
Ah well! as month by month shall wane—
    As passing years shall fade,
Till some of us come back again.
    After our first decade,—

4 So wane the months, so fade the years,
    Where'er our lot may fall,—
That brighter joys and lighter cares
    May be the lot of all.
But while we stand a lingering band,
    The winged moments fail;
We clasp each classmate's parting hand,
    And sing "GOD SAVE OLD YALE."

PARTING ODE.

BY ISAAC RILEY, '58.

Air—"Auld Lang Syne."

1. Should auld acquaintance be forgot,
    And thoughts of days gone by?
Can memories of this hallowed spot,
    And early friendships, die?
While hope shall burn, while life shall last,
    This thought shall never fail—
Sad thought—though sweetest of the past,
    The friends we loved at Yale.

2. Old elms, ye've watched in by-gone years,
    Beneath your garland green,
The glad re-unions and the tears
    Of many a parting scene;
Oh! blest by sweetest airs of heaven!
    Grow high, old elms, and hale,
While we renew the pledges given
    To friends we've loved at Yale.

3. Old walls! round which the thoughts of years
    Now past, so sweetly throng,
Ye soon shall echo with our cheers,
    And hear our parting song,
Old walls! may sunny memories dwell
    Around you, ne'er to fail
Till ye shall hear the last farewell
    Of friends who've loved at Yale.

4. Old friends! we bid a last farewell
    Sad eye, and tear-wet cheek,
Hand clasped in hand, shall truly tell
    The thoughts we may not speak;
To dim this scene, no winter blast,
    Or cloud shall e'er avail,
But hearts shall hold, while life shall last,
    Their love for friends at Yale.

PARTING ODE.

BY EDWARD C. SHEFFIELD, '59.

Air—"Auld Lang Syne."

1. Oh, stern the power that brings the hour,
    To sever hands and hearts;
And sad the chime that marks the time
    Our lingering band departs.
Farewell, where'er around each year
    Bright memories fondly twine;
Farewell the song we loved so long
    In the days of Fifty-nine.

2. A long farewell to dear Old Yale!
    Through darker days to come,
In memory we'll turn to thee,
    Our happy, classic home.

Beside thy gray old walls to-day
    We plant the clustering vine;
Its freshness shows the love that glows
    For thee in Fifty-nine.

3. Old friends and tried, as side by side
    We stand, where never more
The organ's tone shall roll along
    For us—as oft before—
We pledge in hearty kindness yet,
    Within this sacred shrine
Where first we met, we'll ne'er forget
    The friends of Fifty-nine.

4. Dear friends, the way begun to-day
    Not long our feet may tread;
Not many a year of joy or fear,
    Before we join the dead.
But e'er our light go out in night,
    Or evening's sun decline,
We'll lift the cup of kindness up,
    For Yale and Fifty-nine.

WOODEN-SPOON ODE.

BY H. D. CATLIN, '59.

Air—"Integer Vitæ."

1. O Domus præstans, ubi magni et ampli
Vitam agunt læte et studiunt poliri,
Cui favent Musæ; juvenum patrona,
    Almaque Mater.

2. Splendidæ famæ tibi sint honores,
Gloriæque altæ tibi sint favores,
Teque florentem, sapiens tuendi
    Servet Athene.

3. Filii grati tibi nos canemus,
Ante magnorum hic memores virorum,
Arduæque ulmi placido loquuntur
    Nocte susurru.

4. Sæculis multis maneas, diuque
Laurea frontem niteas corona.
O per ætates celebris futura
    MATER YALENSIS!

5. Cochlear lætum! et tibi nunc agamus
Gratias multas, Soboles Yalensis!
Deque te nostri pueri audientes
    Erudientur.

6. Cum Pater Tempus fuerit senilis
Ipse, resque omnes alias ruina
Ceperit: Vivas redivivum in flore
    COCHLEAR INGENS!

WOODEN SPOON LANCIERS.

Arranged by J. M. LANDER.

No. 2.

No. 3.

No. 4.

No. 5. *FINALE.*

Promenade. No. 1.

Promenade. No. 2.

Promenade. No. 3.

Promenade. No. 4.

BIENNIAL-JUBILEE SONG.

BY P. B. PORTER, '67.

AIR—" *Gay and Happy* "

1 Here to-day with joy unmingled,
　　Round the festive board we meet,
　Comrade grasps the hand of comrade,
　　Smiles of gladness each one greet.
　We have toiled and sung together
　　Through these two eventful years,
　And the smiling, golden future
　Still before us bright appears.

Chorus—Now, merry Juniors, fill every glass,
　　　A bumper we'll drink to the noble
　　　　old class,
　　　　　Sixty-seven,
　　　　　Sixty-seven,
　　　Sixty-seven be our song.

2 Many joys and many troubles,—
　　Now Biennial worst and last,—
　We have known and borne together ;
　　Now we bid adieu the past.
　Good bye, spunky girl, Electra,
　　" God-detested thing of hate ;"
　Farewell, sturdy old Prometheus,
　　Buckled down by direful fate.
　　　Chorus.

3 To the big Athenian spouter
　　We, alas, can't say adieu
　For he'll thunder *de corona*,
　　When the Summer weeks are through.
　Good bye, gentle, jolly Horace,
　　Good bye, little Sabine farm.
　"Nocter cœnæque deorum,"
　　Sixty-eight you now will charm.
　　　Chorus.

4 *De honesto et decoro,*
　　O most noble Cicero,
　And of Cato and Panætius,
　　We no more will hear thee blow.
　Farewell, courted, kicked Jejunus,
　　Farewell, wondrous space of fish ;
　Here's to pussy old Montanus,
　　Peace be with him and his dish.
　　　Chorus.

5 Vals, learned Doctor Whately,
　　Still lay on your slander thick—
　Only pile it on quite stoutly,
　　And be sure that some will stick.
　Go to grass, infernal Conics,
　　Litres, metres, ares and steres ;
　Must we part, dear Anna Lytics?
　　Father Day, behold our tears.
　　　Chorus.

6 Buried be whate'er of sorrow,
　　Or of wrong the past has seen ;
　Put, oh, let its joys and pleasures
　　In our memories e'er be green.
　Turn we to the opening future,
　　Bright its visions now loom up ;
　Wooden spoons and ivy plantings—
　　Who will try the silver cup?
　　　Chorus.

PARTING SONG.

BY FRANK H. HOUSTON, '59.

AIR —" *Happy are we to-night, boys.*"

1 Strike up, strike up the song, boys,
　　In unity of heart,
　With joy we meet to-day, boys,
　　In sorrow we must part.
　We gladly cease from constant toil,
　　The years of bondage fled ;
　Yet weep to leave the fostering soil
　　To which our feet are wed.

Chorus—Joyful and sad to-day, boys,
　　　Sad and joyful are we ;
　　　We cast our chains away, boys,
　　　And weep that we are free.

2 No more that Matin bell, boys,
　　Shall break our fondest dreams,
　While long upon the spell, boys,
　　Shall wait the chiding beams ;
　But when we run life's sturdy race,
　　That calls for " main and might,"
　We shall not have each other's face
　　To make our burdens light.

Chorus—Joyful and sad to-day, boys, &c.

3 Now fill the Pipe of Peace, boys,
　　And let the smoke-rings fly,
　To crown the bow with wreathes, boys,
　　And drape the classic sky.
　Our College-days are lit around
　　With sun-set-amber glow—
　Soon must these golden arrows bound
　　Forever from the bow.

Chorus—Joyful and sad to-day, boys,
　　　Sad and joyful are we ;
　　　We cast our chains away, boys,
　　　And weep that we are free.

SONG OF THE SILVER-CUP.

CLASS OF '55.

AIR—"*Benny Havens, O!*"

1 Come join together, classmates, a little song
we'll sing,
About the changes of three years, while
Time's been on the wing,
Of how we once were boys, and though we
now are reckoned men,
Despite the years and growth of cares, we
all are boys again.
We all are boys again, &c.

2 And though we may have been rough shod,
since last we parted here,
Although through tangled ways our path
we may have had to clear,
And though we may have sober grown, since
College boys we came,
Yet looking round us, we are sure our
hearts are just the same.
Our hearts are just the same, &c.

3 There's dignity and stateliness about each
married man,
A sort of "I'm above you," air, "Do like-
wise when you can."—
And some in a paternal way, when asked
what they have done,
Will look a trifle wise, and then present
the little one—
Present the little one, &c.

4 There are Cœlibes among us too,—all growl-
ing at the girls,
Who savage say that every one should
bang in her own curls,
And others of a milder mood, who'd never
like them be,
Are glad to-morrow they can change their
Bachelor's degree!
Their Bachelor's degree, &c.

5 But Bachelors and Benedicks, all think alike
to-night,
We come, a class to greet "our boy," to
see him started right,
Let Livy, Balbus, and Jim Dwight, far back
in memory fall,
Because a little Roman's here, the noblest
of them all!
The noblest of them all, &c.

6 And as we bid the lad "God-speed," and
give to him the cup,
We wish him never to creep down, but
always to climb up;

And as we watch our god-son's course, old
scenes spring up alive,
And once again we live and act, mere
boys of Fifty-five!
Mere boys of Fifty-five!

7 Then let us join each brother's hand, let's
pledge one beaker brimmed,
To the glad brightness of that past whose
lustre is not dimmed,
And as our thoughts will cluster round each
old familiar scene,
We'll live again the dear old time and keep
its memories green—
And keep its memories green, &c.

BIENNIAL JUBILEE SONG.

BY F. B. DEXTER, '61.

AIR— "*Auld Lang Syne.*"

1 While down the stream of life we float,
In careless youthful hours,
Oft on the beach we moor our boat,
And pluck the opening flowers.
So here in harbor, free from care,
Where storms are past, have we
Rejoiced the pipe of peace to share,
In joyful jubilee.

2 As swift as dreams of morning flit,
Two years have told their tale,
Since we the fires of friendship lit
In "classic shades" of Yale:
To-day we've not forgot their claim,
But with devotion true,
At friendship's altar fed the flame,
And plighted love anew.

3 A love whose tie shall reach beyond
The parting now begun,
To seal in after years the bond
Of Yale and Sixty-one!
And in our hearts shall linger long,
No less serenely shine,
When college days we count among
The days of "auld lang syne."

4 Then closely clasp the parting hand,
And warmly say good-bye,
While we by death unsevered stand,
And hopes are beating high;
And as we launch our boats once more
To breast the swelling sea,
We'll treasure up in memory's store
This day of Jubilee!

BIENNIAL JUBILEE SONG.

BY CHAS. H. OWEN, '60.

AIR—"*Nelly Bly.*"

1 Sophs were groaning
And condoling
  Round Alumni Hall,
Tutors thundered
"No 'Old Hundred'
  Should be sung at all."
But a hundred
Voices muttered
  Darkly round the door;
Sad the moan
And deep the groan,
  "Biennials are a bore."

2 They searched our pockets,
Watches, lockets,
  When we all came in;
They watched us, too,
The morning through,
  As though *we* meant "to skin."
But they did'nt
Think a minute
  Of the water jug;
We could keep
A pony leaf,
  In the bottom of the mug.

3 Ladies pretty
Showed up pity
  In Biennial;
But the tutors,
Gallant tutors
  Drove them from the hall;
Then a hundred
Tables thundered
  Banged about the floor,
Sad the moan
And deep the groan,
  "Biennials are a bore!"

4 Tutor spies
Shut their eyes
  When they go to sleep,
Then how spry
The "equali"
  When there's none to peek.
Oh Tutors!
Sleepy Tutors!
  Lots of pony leaves
Rolled up tight,
Out of sight,
  Carried in our sleeves!

5 Now we're Junes,
Jolly Junes,
  Biennial is done,
Nothing now
The whole year thro'
  But jollity and fun.
Sophomore!
Bow before
  Our magnificence!
Freshman brat!
Take off your hat—
  No impertinence!

BIENNIAL-JUBILEE SONG.

BY J. H. TWICHELL, '59.

AIR—"*Happy are we to-night Boys!*"

1 Jovial the song we raise, boys!
Jovial, jovial the song—
Greeting those happier days, boys!
For which no more we long.
A glad farewell to weary toil,
Rings forth our joyous shout:
A merry welcome hails the hour,
With mirth and wassail bout.

  Chorus—Jolly are we to-day, boys!
    Jolly, jolly are we;
    For care hath flown away, boys!
    And Fifty-nine is free.

2 Sophs no longer are we, boys!
Sophs no longer our name:
Voices of Jubilee, boys!
Our Junior days proclaim,
But golden memories, cherished dear,
Around our hearts entwine;
For happy, genial were the hours
Of Sophomore Fifty-nine.   *Chorus.*

3 Quickly the years will fly, boys!
Quickly, quickly the years—
Ere long a sad good-bye, boys!
To all that Yale endears.
The tear and sigh too soon will fall,
And disappointment chill;
But let our band be festive now,
And brimming goblets fill.   *Chorus.*

4 Fill up! Fill up! to Yale, boys!
Fill up! to Fifty-nine,
Our Junior freedom hail, boys!
Fill high the sparkling wine!
On Alma Mater's noble brow,
Long may her laurels rest;
And long may "Yale" a watch-word be,
To thrill the student breast.   *Chorus.*

BIENNIAL-JUBILEE SONG.

BY B. K. PHELPS, '53.

AIR—"*Sparkling and Bright*"

1 Happy and gay are our hearts to-day,
  And our footsteps fall full lightly;
For Biennial bore is now no more,
  And Junior hopes shine brightly.
    The loud prolong the joyous song,
    In a hearty swelling chorus—
    For the sunlight clear of our Junior
        year
    Is beaming bright before us.

2 How much helped us the *equulus*,
  That we brought in our pockets slily;
While with jealous care we escaped the stare
  Of the tutor's gaze so wily.

3 See the downcast air, and the blank despair,
  That sits on each Soph'more feature,
As his bleared eyes gleam o'er that horrid
      scheme!
  He's sure a wretched creature.

4 Yet there still remains, in all his pains,
  One drop of consolation;—
He heeds not the knell of the morning bell,
  That wakes the College nation.

5 The Rubicon passed, we look back at last
  O'er our two years thronged with pleas-
      ures,—
Yet a tear will fall as we pace the hall
  Where mem'ry hoards her treasures.

6 But the days to come in our College home,
  Are full of joy and glory,
And FIFTY-THREE for aye shall be
  The theme of many a story.

7 Then three loud cheers for the pleasant
      years
  That await us still in College,
And *nine* for the Class which none may
      surpass
  For freedom fun or knowledge.

BROTHERS IN UNITY—RE-UNION SONG.

BY JOHN. M. HOLMES, '63.

AIR—"*Sparkling and Bright.*"

1 Mingle we here, old Brothers dear,
  The true—the happy hearted,
To dream of the prime of that student time,
  When we were yet unparted.

Chorus— Then, Brothers, shout the chorus
          out,
Bis.   In glad and grateful greeting,
          As we used to do when the bright
          hours flew,
          And we heeded not their fleeting.

2 Richer than gold are those memories old,
  That thrill our souls with pleasure,
For rust nor stealth can waste the wealth
  Of love's eternal treasure.

  Chorus—Bis.

3 A nod and a smile for a little while,
  As friends we give to others,
But the quivering lip and the good old grip,
  Proclaim that *we* are BROTHERS.

  Chorus—Bis.

4 Full many a name well known to fame,
  Were Brothers here before us,
And the old blue flag which our fathers had,
  Still floats in triumph o'er us.

  Chorus—Bis.

5 Now side by side, in joy and pride,
  As Brothers tried and truthful,
Around the shrine of "auld lang syne,"
  Once more let all be youthful.

  Chorus—Bis.

6 And when life's ray shall fade away,
  To evening's gentle warning,
'Twill still point back on manhood's track,
  To a spot where all was morning.

  Chorus—Bis.

INDEX OF FIRST LINES.